Prepare to Answer

Prepare to Answer

A Defense of the Christian Faith

Rubel Shelly

BAKER BOOK HOUSE
Grand Rapids, Michigan 49516

Copyright 1990 by
Baker Book House Company

ISBN: 0-8010-8307-9

Second printing, May 1990

Printed in the United States of America

To
The Family of God at Woodmont Hills
a colony of believers
in an unbelieving world

Contents

Acknowledgments

My thanks to Russ Gough and Randy Harris for using the original manuscript of this book as a text in their apologetics courses at David Lipscomb University. The field testing provided by their use of it and the student feedback they passed along helped clarify some obtuse passages.

Thanks also to Tom Eddins for his personal reading, critique, and helpful suggestions on the final draft of *Prepare to Answer*.

Finally, a special thanks to Diana Gilfilen for her patient and careful preparation of the manuscript from first draft to final form. My work is made significantly easier by her competence.

Introduction

I believe in God, the infinite, personal, Spirit reality who has existed eternally and who has brought all things other than himself into being and who always acts in harmony with his perfect and unchanging nature.

I believe in Jesus Christ, the historical figure of Nazareth, as the personal revelation of deity in human form and as the one and only means of access human beings have into the fellowship of God.

I believe in the Bible as the propositional revelation of God to his human creatures; in it God has used words to make known to us his holy will, which focuses on Jesus, to give us direction for right living and to point us to heaven.

I believe in man as the creation of God, that every man and woman of whatever race or geographical location on Planet Earth bears the image of God in his or her being and is responsible to God to glorify him in all things.

These are incredibly bold affirmations. Yet they have been made so often in the presence of so many people that some Christians are altogether casual and even blasé about them. Unbelievers and skeptics might say that such claims are "absurd" or "nonsensical." Unless those of us who affirm these things do so with zeal and back them up with committed discipleship, it is unlikely that anyone will take particular notice of them.

So bold a confession of Christian faith demands a willingness to offer justification for these beliefs and implies an openness to questioning and challenge concerning them. The recent retreat into pious subjectivism by many "Christian confessors" is unworthy of anyone who values intellectual and spiritual integrity.

I do not blush or cringe when I say that I embrace the Christian religion and affirm its foundational doctrines concerning God, Christ, Scripture, and mankind. Such a confession is neither antiintellectual in posture nor unworthy of critical thinkers from disciplines ranging from the sciences to philosophy to just plain "common sense." The studies to be undertaken in this book relate to the legitimacy of a Christian's affirmations of faith. I cannot come to these topics and claim neutrality. I am *not* neutral; I am a committed believer. But I can pledge to be intellectually honest in the pursuit ahead.

One does not have to be without a commitment in a matter in order to think and act with integrity. I am hardheaded enough that I must be honest with my own intellect in tracing out any subject. It is not in my nature to be able to say, "It's grand to believe so-and-so," while my mind has reservations about it. At an earlier time in my life, doubts and unresolved questions caused me to be skeptical about the things I now affirm with confidence. Those uncertainties forced me to study, test, explore, and challenge. The result has been faith. But it would have been antagonism toward Christianity if the evidence had been lacking.

Some of the formulations, proofs, and defenses put forth for certain elements of the Christian faith by some would-be apologists are incredibly poor. No one without a pre-established bias in favor of the position in question could possibly be convinced by them. They are weak and embarrassing. If people think such poor arguments are the best that Christians have to offer, I can understand why some are unbelievers.

This book demonstrates a willingness to examine counterclaims and points to problem areas pertaining to the formulation and defense of Christian tenets. I try to make only such claims as can be backed up by the facts placed in evidence.

There is nothing wrong with thinking, asking hard questions, and demanding rigorous examination of claims. It is not ungodly, pagan, or wicked to ask for justification of Christianity's truth claims. And there is certainly no virtue in denying the doubt or confusion that may arise in one's mind. The only honest thing to do with a doubt is to surface it, face it squarely, and attempt to resolve it.

I do not make fun of people who are struggling with doubt. To the contrary, my own past experience causes me to feel a strong sense of empathy with them. From my own probing and searching, I have learned that faith has nothing to fear from honest and serious investigation. It turns out that faith only glows brighter for the rubbing.

This book, then, grows out of my own background and personal studies. I hope it is something you will find challenging and interesting for the sake of your own study. No attempt is being made here to give a course in philosophy or to write a book in the technical jargon of academics. Every effort will be made to deal with the issues of Christian apologetics in language that can be handled by people from many backgrounds who lack the training of a specialist in the field. After all, these are issues of vital concern to all people. They can never be isolated and made the exclusive domain of "professionals." It would be unpardonable naiveté to think that "the common man" cannot concern himself with subjects of such magnitude. Not only *may* he address himself to the issues of theism, the deity of Jesus, inspiration, and man as a created being, he *must* do so.

Having promised to deal with the issues of Christian apologetics in simplified language, I should also note that these are profound themes that will require concentration and mental effort on the part of the reader. Once-over-lightly reading of these chapters will not be sufficient to follow what is being offered. Careful reading, attention to the interconnectedness of issues, and a willingness to think critically will be necessary if this study is to yield significant benefit to those who begin it.

Obviously, I believe the theoretical aspect of Christianity is necessary, worth articulating carefully, and capable of defense in the face of attack. Otherwise why this book? But beginning or would-be apologists need to be warned that there are barriers to faith that are other than intellectual. This will help them present their case more effectively. This will also help them deal with the inevitable rejection that will come from some.

Rejection, when it does come, may be due neither to the message you have articulated nor to your manner of presentation, but to a much deeper, personal wound that you cannot yet see or understand in a person. In such cases of rejection, continue to befriend the person, show respect, and wait for a later opportunity to share your faith. Don't try to force the message down anyone's throat with a forked stick. That would justify the prejudice that person already harbors against Christians.

Show love, gentleness, and patience. Allow the Spirit of God to bring his power and providences to bear. Wait for the soil to be properly prepared for the good seed you are sowing.

Let's get about the task of apologetics. Whether you read this book as a Christian seeking help in sharing and defending the faith, or as a skeptic or unbeliever willing to take a look at the case believers make, we have an exciting series of issues to examine.

RUBEL SHELLY

1

Thinkers *Can* Be Believers

Before sitting down to write a book, one should have a purpose in mind. I had a clear purpose in mind as I wrote this book, and it may help you in reading it to know what that purpose was. Then, as you read, you may check the book's progress against its clearly stated objective.

The purpose of this book is indicated by its title, *Prepare to Answer: A Defense of the Christian Faith*. It attempts to collect in one volume some of the strong reasons for believing in the God of the Bible, for accepting the Old and New Testaments as his verbal communication of truth to humanity, and for believing that God came among human beings in the person of Jesus of Nazareth.

This book certainly makes no claim to contain *all* of the proofs that could be offered for Christianity. The ones presented are the ones that impress me most and that seem to be of most interest to people with whom I have studied these issues. At crucial points, arguments thought by some to count against the Christian faith will be presented and examined.

I have attempted to be faithful to the Christian obligation stated in these words from the New Testament: "Always be prepared to give an answer to everyone who asks you to give the reason for the hope that you have" (1 Peter 3:15b). This explicit duty of offering reasons for holding the Christian faith puts the religion of Jesus Christ in a unique category. Its principal appeal is not that it will make life pleasant or solve all of society's problems, but that *it is true*. This appeal puts Christianity into the public marketplace of ideas, invites critical investigation, and implies a willingness to make a clearheaded case for itself.

It is assumed that the people willing to offer a reasoned defense of Christian faith are themselves believers: "But in your hearts set apart Christ as Lord" (1 Peter 3:15a). Yet a believer must be fair, open-minded, and honest. That is, he or she must avoid naive dogmatism and face up to the hard questions without pretending they don't exist or simply throwing up a smokescreen of platitudes. Folding one's hands and looking pious is not a sufficient answer to an honest, but hard, question.

It is also assumed that the person defending Christian faith will do so in the spirit of Christ: "But do this with gentleness and respect" (1 Peter 3:15c). Jesus was not a bully. He did not insult the intelligence or character of people who asked sincere questions. Some who have undertaken to defend Christian faith have not always followed his example of gentle and respectful treatment of unbelievers. Their harsh manner has likely turned some away from Christianity who could have been convinced by facts presented with greater kindness.

The final preliminary point along this line is to identify the specific subject matter up for discussion in this book. Having defined the word *defense* from the title, let me now say a bit about the term *Christian faith*. As I am using it, the term refers to the fundamental doctrines of Christianity—the existence of the personal God of the Bible, his incarnation in the person of Jesus of Nazareth, and the trustworthiness of the Old and New Testaments as written revelation of the divine will for humanity. Essential corollaries of these doctrines would include the exclusivity of the Christian religion as the means of coming to God for eternal life and the presentation of Jesus of Nazareth as the one and only Savior of mankind.

In addition to these fundamental beliefs of historic Christianity, there are many other items of biblical interpretation and personal faith that I hold. My role as a "Christian apologist" (a technical term for one who offers a reasoned defense of Christianity) does not obligate me to defend any particular expression of Christian faith within a certain denomination or sect. My obligation is confined to basic Christian beliefs and does not extend to millennial theories, church organization, and the like. These are important in due course, but they are not the foundational issues of the Christian faith. Neither am I committed to defend the wicked things that people have done in the name of Christianity through the centuries—whether the Spanish Inquisition or a personal sin in my life. The truth or falsity of Christian faith is a separate issue from the faithfulness or unfaithfulness of its adherents in practicing it.

Every attempt has been made to keep the language of the book simple. There are times and places to write very technical articles and books for scholars in this field, but this book is not intended for that audience. The person of average intelligence who has an interest in the topics treated here will be able to read profitably. At the same time, since these are challenging issues, some of the reading will have to be done at an unhurried pace and with close attention. Anything this important both demands and deserves some mental energy.

In this first chapter, the crucial issue is to understand something about the nature of faith. When someone says, "I believe that Jesus Christ is the Son of God," how shall we understand that statement? Is it best understood as an affirmation of certainty about the identity of Jesus of Nazareth? Or does the word *believe* imply a degree of doubt? How is "believing" related to "knowing"? Suppose someone asked the person who made that statement to explain why. What sorts of reasons (justification) are appropriate to belief statements?

These are important questions, and different people might answer them very differently. Let me explain the approach this book will take to answering them.

What Is Faith?

We use the equivalent expressions "I believe so-and-so" or "I have faith that so-and-so" in a variety of ways. Consider the following:

(a) "I believe the Earth is flat."
(b) "I believe the Steelers will go to the Super Bowl."
(c) "I believe you are wearing my jacket."
(d) "I believe Harry Truman was a lifelong Republican."
(e) "I believe George Washington was our first president."
(f) "I believe it is your turn to carry out the garbage."
(g) "I believe in Margaret."

These statements all present themselves as faith statements, but they are very different from one another. At least one of them is what most of us would call a *credulous belief* (a). At least one of them is *mere belief*, opinion, or "wishful thinking" (b, possibly c or f). At least one statement has the potential for being called a *substantive belief* (e, possibly c, f, or g). At least one is a *mistaken belief* (d, possibly a, b, c, f, or g). At least one of them is a *true and justified belief* (e, possibly c or f). And one of them is a statement of *personal trust* (g).

A *credulous belief* is one with little or nothing to commend it to people of average intelligence and common sense. The notion of a flat Earth certainly seems to qualify as such a belief today. Inductive evidence has led long ago to the consensus belief that the Earth was a spheroid. More recently we have had satellite photographs and eyewitness reports from astronauts to confirm that view. The fact that a belief has no rational support does not mean, however, that no one holds it. There is an International Flat Earth Society that insists that the supposed proofs of a spherical Earth are falsified.

A *mere belief* is one that rests on rather flimsy evidence, may be unduly influenced by personal desire, or may be the projection of a fantasy. Partisan loyalty to a team causes many a fan to believe in championship possibilities prior to the start of every season. Laziness may make a sibling believe it is someone else's turn to do a household chore. The fact that a piece of clothing looks like one you own may or may not mean that it really is yours; more checking (looking at the label) can verify or disprove the belief.

A _substantive belief_ is one with good enough justification that it would take very strong contrary evidence to cause a person to abandon it. Or, to say it another way, it is a belief held on the basis of such good evidence that other fair-minded persons may be persuaded to share it. It is remotely possible that we have been misinformed about the first president of the United States—but not likely. It would take overwhelming evidence to move me away from my strong belief that George Washington was our first chief executive.

Or take the case of the jacket again. Suppose you own a jacket with a rather distinctive stain on the left sleeve. You put it on a hanger in the den when you came home one day. Sometime later, while fixing a snack in the kitchen, you see John walk in from the den, wearing what appears to be your jacket. You can see the distinctive stain, so you say, "I believe you are wearing my jacket." "Yes," he says, "I am going to bring in the newspaper. Do you mind if I borrow it for a minute?" Your belief is confirmed, and you give permission for him to borrow your jacket. Case closed. But suppose he says, "No. This is mine." You protest that it looks just like your own, right down to the stain on the left sleeve. You may even begin to feel upset. Why is John trying to make off with your jacket? So you ask him to go into the den with you so you can check the coat rack for your jacket. And there is your jacket, right where you left it! You pull it down and show John how similar they are—even to the stains on the left sleeves. You had good reason to think he had your jacket, but you are now convinced that you made a mistake.

A *mistaken belief* is not unheard of among fallible human beings. The case of the jacket described above illustrates how beliefs can be wrong. A beginning history student, learning the nation's presidents, may get the order wrong on a test. Or he may assign Truman, Eisenhower, or Kennedy to the wrong political party. It happens all the time. Just recall some tests you took in school. Or ask a high school history teacher.

We do not typically speak of "false knowledge," but the expression "false belief" is a familiar one. For example, the sentence "Teresa holds the false *belief* that Rio de Janiero is in Africa" makes sense; the sentence "Teresa holds the false *knowledge* that Rio de Janiero is in Africa" makes no sense at all. It is linguistically and rationally correct to say "false belief"; "false knowledge" is simply incorrect and does not qualify as "knowledge" of any sort.

More will be said later about the relationship between faith and knowledge. Here it is enough to say that all knowledge entails belief, but not all belief entails knowledge. Sound complex? Not really. Take the jacket episode again. The fact that you believed John was wearing your jacket in no way guaranteed the correctness of that belief; you may have believed it so, but you obviously did not know it. On the other hand, if you know from experience that water at sea level boils at 100 degrees Celsius, you are certainly justified in saying, "I believe water at sea level will boil at 100 degrees Celsius." Knowledge of a fact justifies faith statements about it; faith statements do not guarantee their truthfulness. This will be an important point to come back to later.

A *true and justified belief* is the sort of faith statement that earns the name "knowledge." In fact, philosophers define knowledge in terms of precisely these three elements: (1) truth, (2) belief, and (3) justification. First, you could never "know" that water boils at 0 degrees Celsius, for it simply is not so. One can only know what is actually true. Second, before you could personally claim to know a given fact, you would have to assert belief in it. For example, even if it is true that Calvin Coolidge was the thirtieth president of the United States, you would not be said to know that fact if it were nowhere in your system of beliefs and affirmations. Third, you can know a given fact (as opposed to merely guessing or hoping it is so) only if you have a good reason for believing it to be so. In the case of the Coolidge presidency, consulting an encyclopedia would usually be adequate justification; in the case of water boiling at 100 degrees Celsius, a laboratory experiment would be your best reason for claiming to know the fact.

Among the statements above, "I believe George Washington was our first president" qualifies as a true and justified belief. One who has studied a bit of history would probably simply assert that "George Washington was our first president" or might even say, "I am certain that George Washington was our first president."

Not all true beliefs are justified in the same way. Whereas questions about the American presidency could be settled by checking an encyclopedia or history book, neither of those sources would help you know whose turn it is to carry out the garbage at your house. You would check a schedule or search your memory to recall who did the job last and then assign today's chore. Checking to find whose jacket that is or why you "believe in Margaret" would be done in still other ways.

An affirmation of *personal trust* is a rather special form of faith statement. It moves from the realm of cold, hard facts to warm, personal relationships. Even so, there is a clear relationship between facts and trust.

Previous experience with Margaret being truthful with you forms the basis for taking her word now. Her consistent honesty in handling money for a community theater group you belong to allows you to recommend her for a job at a bank. Her willingness to stand by you through some personal crisis makes you confident about asking her help in a new time of stress. The accumulated factual experiences you have shared with Margaret make possible the affirmation of absolute confidence in her.

Where to Place Christian Beliefs

We must place Christian beliefs somewhere along the continuum traced above. But where?

Some make it clear that they consider belief in the God of the Bible a credulous belief. In the introduction to a book attacking theism, one writer said his purpose in the book was

> . . . to demonstrate that the belief in god is irrational to the point of absurdity; and that this irrationality, when manifested in specific religions such as Christianity, is extremely harmful. . . . If a person wishes to continue believing in a god, that is his prerogative, but he can no longer excuse his belief in the name of reason and moral necessity.[1]

Others insist that Christian beliefs are mere beliefs without any hard evidence in their favor. An atheist of a century ago explained God as a magnified image of man that man has projected onto the universe. Some have explained God as a psychological fantasy invented by insecure creatures who needed a cosmic father to hold them on his lap and reassure them.

It seems quite popular today to hold that religious beliefs have nothing in common with reasoned inquiry and stand immune to proof or disproof. Thus the following in an editorial from a major American newspaper: "Systems of belief and tenets of faith are powerful in men's minds, but, by their very nature, do not lend themselves to proof."[2] Or this from a national news magazine: "Faith is belief without reason. Fundamentally, religions oppose rational processes, perhaps on the theory that a God who could be approached by mere rational thought would not be worth reaching."[3]

I reject both of these interpretations of the nature of Christian faith. I am too hardheaded and rational a person to embrace something with my heart that my mind thinks untrue. I could never encourage anyone to accept the

Christian religion against the weight of the evidence. Here I would quote with endorsement the words of an atheist:

> It is my firm conviction that man has nothing to gain, emotionally or otherwise, by adhering to a falsehood, regardless of how comfortable or sacred that falsehood may appear. Anyone who claims, on the one hand, that he is concerned with human welfare, and who demands, on the other hand, that man must suspend or renounce the use of his reason, is contradicting himself. . . . To advocate irrationality is to advocate that which is destructive to human life.[4]

If the force of the evidence is against Christian beliefs, they should be rejected. The recent tendency to redefine faith as the acceptance of things for which there is no proof is both contradictory to and destructive of the Christian religion. To speak of the need for a "leap of faith," by which one brings himself to accept what his reason thinks is unsupported (and, perhaps, unsupportable), is irrational and unchristian. If it is legitimate to believe Christian tenets in spite of the evidence, it is equally justified to believe anything one wishes "by faith."

The view of faith sustained throughout the Bible is against shallow, emotional commitments (of the sort sometimes sought in Christian circles) and on the side of only such commitments as are considered and rational.

Christian faith finds its meaning in its truthfulness. It is always open to rational discussion and offers to set forth a case for the unbeliever to consider (1 Peter 3:15). Biblical Christianity is not assent to church-approved dogma, whether it be true or not. Real Christianity is assent to truth, whatever that truth may be.

One who takes the time to read through the Book of Acts to see how the earliest Christians presented the message of Christ is impressed that their preaching did not bypass the understanding but enlightened it. Rather than mystical speculation or emotional appeals, it was always an appeal first to the mind with a view toward engaging the will in seeking an enlightened response to the will of God.

Minimally, then, Christianity is held throughout this volume to be either a substantive belief (one with weightier evidence for it than against it) or mistaken belief. A third category of "mistaken-yet-legitimate beliefs" seems to insult rationality and smack of reducing all belief systems to meaninglessness.

Christian belief statements are actually *truth claims* that take a consistent form. Thus, "I believe in Jesus Christ" is not equivalent to "I agree to follow Jesus Christ, whether he was real or mythical, worked miracles or was regarded with superstitious awe by gullible people, or rose bodily from the dead or not." Rather, "I believe in Jesus Christ" translates to "I claim to have adequate justification for making the truth claim that Jesus Christ is the incomparable Son of God and for looking to him as my Savior."

Unlike the mythical religions of the Greeks and Romans, the Christian religion is grounded in historical events with real content and dynamic import for human lives. Those events are subject to the same type of historical inquiries we use to ascertain the truth about Socrates, Alexander the Great, or Franklin D. Roosevelt. The sacred volume purporting to record those events is open to the same critical scrutiny as the dialogues of Plato or the alleged diaries of Adolf Hitler. The epistemology and ethic of Jesus Christ must face the same philosophic tests of coherence and pragmatic value that we press on those of other thinkers.

Beyond the minimal level of substantive belief, Christian faith can be affirmed even more strongly as true and justified belief. Here we may expect to meet some hesitation, even among those who may be inclined toward sympathy with the stated purpose of this book. Since a true and justified belief is what we label "knowledge," it is now being claimed that Christian faith can be held as a matter of knowledge. Is this claiming too much? Are not faith and knowledge different spheres?

Remember the point made earlier about the relationship between faith and knowledge: "All knowledge entails belief, but not all belief entails knowledge." Belief and knowledge are certainly not mutually exclusive, for anything that one knows is also a part of his belief system. The very definition of knowledge that is traditionally used (true and justified *belief*) affirms a relationship between the two. What one believes to be the case can be so adequately confirmed to him that he will be willing to say that he not only believes so-and-so, but knows it to be a fact.

The factors that allow one to move from the level of strong affirmation (substantive belief) to that of professed certainty (true and justified belief = knowledge) involve both intellectual and psychological elements. Thus, a woman's increasing confidence that her critically ill child is improving may be influenced not only by test results and physicians' assurances, but also by her optimistic personality and her ability to "read" her baby. This works the other way, too. Since some mothers are pessimistic and tend to panic in a crisis, objective data that the child is recovering may do very little, in that case, to relieve her fears or give her hope.

To admit that factors other than objective data enter into one's degree of certainty about a matter is not to say that objective matters are not primary. It is simply to admit what we all know. Some people seem rather naturally inclined to religious convictions by virtue of background and temperament, while others are extremely skeptical. The former must be warned against going beyond the data, and the latter must be cautioned against requiring more proof than is reasonable.

Faith is not less than genuine when it seeks additional confirmation. Scripture itself speaks of "little faith" and "great faith." And Jesus did not chide Thomas for insisting on confirmation of the ten other apostles' testimony that Jesus had risen from the dead. He offered himself for Thomas to touch his hands and side, saying, "Stop doubting and believe" (John 20:27c). Of special interest are Jesus' other words to him: "Because you have seen me, you have believed; blessed are those who have not seen and yet have believed" (John 20:29).

Some have thought it impossible for modern believers to have faith comparable to that of eyewitnesses to Jesus' life and miracles. But think about it. Not everyone who was an eyewitness believed his claims. And most of us who were not eyewitnesses to any of the events in the lives of Julius Caesar, Susan B. Anthony, or Joseph Stalin have no problem believing the primary reports we have of their lives. Contemporaries expect and demand one sort of proof, and people coming along later expect and demand proof of another sort. When the appropriate proof is forthcoming to either group, faith is adequately justified for each.

That faith can, at least under certain circumstances, be so strong as to become knowledge is supported by Peter's statement: "We believe and know that you are the Holy One of God" (John 6:69). Similar statements are still common among people of all backgrounds. Suppose you ask if I believe my wife truly loves me. I would likely reply, "I not only believe she loves me; I know it."

That Christian faith can (and, ideally, will) rise to the strongest level of affirmation is clear from this verse: "Now faith is being sure of what we hope for and certain of what we do not see" (Heb. 11:1). Faith grows, deepens, and solidifies with the accumulation of additional data supporting it, with mature reflection on the nature and content of biblical revelation, and with experiential confirmation through a daily walk with Jesus as Lord.

It is in this last matter (experiential confirmation through a daily walk with Jesus as Lord) that a "special form of faith statement" becomes intelligible. There is the matter of personal trust.

Since it is the closest human relationship in my experience and gives a basis for communicating an important matter, let me illustrate personal trust by saying more about my wife. When I tell you that "I believe in Myra," I have gone far beyond both "substantive faith" and "true, justified beliefs" (knowledge) about her person and character. I mean that everything I am and all that I possess is at her disposal. I am willing to trust her about things that I have had no way to confirm for myself. The past twenty-five years of confident, loving relationship with her allow me to take her word for things that I will never bother to check. Of course, that kind of faith in another person makes one very vulnerable, and it has been known to be abused from one person to another.

When a Christian says, "I believe in Jesus Christ," he is saying more than, "I have more positives than negatives in my mind about Jesus." He is even moving to a level of affirmation that goes beyond the courtroom's certainty-beyond-reasonable-doubt. He is making himself vulnerable to Christ, putting all that he has and is at his disposal, and trusting him to give meaning to his life. Yes, there is a subjectivity at this level that cannot be fitted into a syllogistic argument.

Unbelievers occasionally like to take swipes at us theists because we believe in a person we can't see. "Show me God!" comes the demand. "Let me hear his voice or touch him," says another.

Perhaps only now can I make clear to you why so much has been said about the nature of our belief structures. Let me remind you again: _Everybody believes in persons, events, and things he has not and cannot see._ As a matter of fact, the overwhelming majority of things you hold as items of knowledge relate to unrepeatable events of history you did not see for yourself and unwitnessable events of the microscopic world that underlie the reality perceived at a commonsense level of day-to-day life. Who was the first president of the U.S.A? Who killed Abraham Lincoln? Who was the teacher of Aristotle? How are thought processes happening right now? What is an electron?

In contrast to what some people think, my opinion is that the greatest confirmation of the right to believe in unseen things is modern science. No one has more faith in an unseen world than a physicist. In order to understand the things we experience with our five senses at a macroscopic level, scientists have built laboratories, read carefully calibrated instruments, performed mathematical calculations, and trusted the logic of their methodology to take them to conclusions that stagger the mind and defy the normal sensory experiences we have in the world of daily events. When a physicist tries to tell me about the subatomic world and quantum physics, for example, I think I sense something of what an unbeliever must feel in listening to us Christians talk about God—a sense of awe and occasional bewilderment.

The ancient Greeks thought the world was made up of varying combinations of four elements: earth, air, fire, and water. More enlightened scientists advanced our understanding of the cosmos to an atomic theory, which saw everything made up of tiny billiard-ball particles called atoms. These atoms variously stuck to, bounced off, or slid over one another to produce solids, gases, and liquids. Later still, the march of science invited us to see atoms no longer as tiny billiard balls but as microscopic versions of the solar system, with their nuclei holding whirling electrons in precise orbits. All these tiny structures were held to comply strictly with the same laws of mechanics that hold the planets in their orbits or guide bullets to their targets.

In the 1920s, however, things were thrown into chaos by a revolution in our understanding of atomic structure. (One wonders what new models will be in the textbooks only a few years away! Few think the last words have yet been spoken on the subject.) The so-called commonsense beliefs about physics that had been held to that point were overthrown. And lest you think that such topics are heavyhanded and impractical, I would remind you of the brilliant practical advances that have come of this revolution: laser, electron microscopes, transistors, nuclear power, and so forth.

The momentous leap of the 1920s has a name: quantum theory. The notion of tiny particles governed by predictable mechanical principles went out the window. The idea of material objects made up of concrete entities gave way to what one writer described as "a maelstrom of fleeting, ghostly images." Niels Bohr, a Danish physicist who was involved in these early discoveries, made this comment about the radical nature of the new departure in physics: "Anyone who is not shocked by quantum theory has not understood it."

Few people *do* understand quantum theory, and I am not one of them. But my response to the sorts of things college freshmen learn about atomic theory in their first physics class is fairly typical. It doesn't seem to make sense; it boggles the mind; it makes me skeptical of the whole field of study called "physics." But my initial bewilderment doesn't mean it isn't true. It only means that I am staggered by something I don't comprehend.

For example, suppose we pursue the first step in modern physics concerning the nature of atomic particles.

> At the heart of the subject lies the bald question: is an atom a *thing*, or just an abstract construct of imagination useful for explaining a wide range of observations? If an atom *really* exists as an independent entity then at the very least it should have a location and a definite motion. But the quantum theory denies this. It says that you can have one or the other but not both.[5]

According to my physicist friend, a subatomic particle such as an electron has either a precise velocity or a precise position, but not both at the same time. (I scratch my head when he tells me things like this.) It is related to a "rule" (?) called the Heisenberg Uncertainty Principle. The more certain one is of the electron's speed, the more uncertain one is of its location and vice versa.

The reason for all this, he tells me, is that electrons in flight cannot be observed. This is not due to instrument problems, but follows from what we understand about the very nature of things at the subatomic level. If an electron's velocity is measured, it simply does not have a location.

"Do you mean to tell me, Albert, that modern science builds its entire house on a foundation of unseen entities?" I ask in amazement.

"That's it!" says he with a wink. "These basic particles of our universe are unknowable to us except through their observable effects and our logical reasoning concerning them."

"I never knew how much alike theists and physicists are," say I, "and will never again be intimidated by the scoffing of someone who chides my faith in unseen things."

The key here has to do with what Albert called "observable effects" and "logical reasoning" concerning those events. One's beliefs may emerge with genuine validity if they avoid the extremes of gullibility and skepticism, if they explain things with coherent force, and if they pass the tests of reason.

> If we are to admit [a subatomic particle's] existence, we can do so only because of its effect on other things. Of course our reasons for believing in the existence of neutrinos are quite different from our reasons for believing in the existence of God or the soul. But if we admit indirect arguments for the existence of neutrinos from the behavior of observable material objects, no amount of ingenuity has so far succeeded in logically ruling out the possibility of arguments for God or the soul on the basis of the behavior of observable objects.[6]

Christian theism is a rational belief if, and only if, it is based on observable effects in this physical world that we contact through the senses and on logical reasoning about those phenomena. My conviction is that Christian theism is more than adequately grounded for rational thinkers. More than that, I admit to some degree of consternation when an otherwise rational thinker tells me that he does not believe in God.

Frankly, I think the failure of people to believe in God is not due to either their stupidity or the inadequacy of evidence available. It is, in my opinion, generally due to (1) the failure of theists such as myself to present the evidence carefully, rationally, and effectively, or (2) the failure of theists such as myself to exhibit the kind of character that unbelievers (legitimately) expect people who profess faith in a holy God to display. When we Christians are prejudiced, dogmatic, and irrational in our beliefs and behavior, we discredit the whole belief system for which we allege to stand.

From the start of this book, then, I want it clearly understood that the faith I am discussing and defending is not the sort that causes people to talk about travel in UFOs, angels dancing on pinheads, or leprechauns. I am talking about faith that is rooted in reason, evidence, and proofs.

In his famous essay, English mathematician and skeptic, William K. Clifford chided religionists of his time for their tendency to accept too much on too little evidence. To the degree that everyone is guilty of committing the error Clifford identified, a rational believer would agree with his rigorous criticism. After denouncing the "habit of believing for unworthy reasons," he concludes:

> To sum up: it is wrong always, everywhere, and for anyone, to believe anything upon insufficient evidence.
> If a man, holding a belief which he was taught in childhood or persuaded of afterwards, keeps down and pushes away any doubts which arise about it in his mind, purposely avoids the reading of books and the company of men that call in question or discuss it, and regards as impious those questions which cannot easily be asked without disturbing it—the life of that man is one long sin against mankind.[7]

The Judeo-Christian religion does not ask people to believe things that are irrational or unevidenced. To be

sure, the evidences relevant to God's existence or the deity
of Christ are not of the sort a physicist studies in his laboratory. They are more generally philosophical arguments,
historical data, and critical examinations into testimony.
The research techniques usually do not involve test tubes
and electron microscopes but the methodology of historians and philosophers. The testing methods some skeptics
insist on applying to the evidences of Christianity are such
that, if applied generally, they would bring into question
the existence of Aristotle and the military campaigns of
Julius Caesar.

Christian faith does not involve believing things without
evidence and is not opposed to reason.

Value and Limits of Reasoned Proofs

The value of reasoned proofs about God's existence, the
inspiration of Scripture, and the deity of Jesus is admittedly limited. The God at the end of a philosopher's argument
is less than the personal God of Abraham; the Bible whose
authenticity and reliability have been demonstrated from
archaeology and predictive prophecy is still a written communication awaiting the opportunity to guide a misdirect-
ed life; and the Jesus who is proved divine by many incontestable proofs cannot save the person who will not confess
and claim him as Savior.

A successful defense of the Christian faith does not
guarantee that God's purpose will be served in the life of
the presenter or his student. Arguments don't save people.
Only a personal relationship with God through Christ can
accomplish that.

What, then, is the value of Christian apologetics? The
philosophical, historical, and biblical arguments of the
apologist can bring people to the brink of salvation and
confront them with that option. Those arguments can
remove obstacles that have stood in the way of someone's
fair hearing of Jesus' offer of eternal life. They can prepare
someone to hear and receive the gospel.

Conclusion

In his famous *Through the Looking-Glass*, logician Lewis Carroll constructs an interesting dialogue between Alice and the White Queen:

> "Now I'll give *you* something to believe. I'm just one hundred and one, five months and a day."
> "I can't believe *that*!" said Alice.
> "Can't you?" the Queen said in a pitying tone. "Try again: draw a long breath, and shut your eyes."
> Alice laughed. "There's no use trying," she said: "One *can't* believe impossible things."
> I daresay you haven't had much practice," said the Queen. "When I was your age, I always did it for half-an-hour a day. Why, sometimes I've believed as many as six impossible things before breakfast."[8]

I agree with Alice and stand against the White Queen's invitation to "believe impossible things." Every time we allow ourselves to believe things without sufficient reason, we diminish our dignity as human beings. We play dishonest games with our rational powers.

In the successive chapters of this book, I will ask only that you follow closely and think clearly. I will ask you to believe nothing without good evidence.

2

God's Fingerprints

The first thing any human being becomes aware of is his or her surroundings. There is a world external to me. It was here before I came on the scene and gives every evidence that it will be here long after I leave. It does not depend on me for its function. In fact, it sometimes functions in ways that cause me problems. But whatever else that world is for me, it is a *factual reality* that I bump into every day.

Babies are conscious of people and things around them long before they are self-conscious. All through life, we remain acutely aware of an objectively real world that we encounter through the sensory experiences of sight, touch, taste, hearing, and smell. It is there. It invites investigation. More than that, our minds force us to think about its origin.

Very early in life, we begin asking ourselves (and others) how our external world came to be there. At first the question may be put very simply, and a few words will probably be sufficient to satisfy us.

"Daddy, how did all the stars get up in the sky?"

A Christian will probably say something like this: "God made them and put them in the sky for your eyes to enjoy."

A non-Christian may say something akin to this: "They

came from a big, fiery explosion in space several billion years ago."

Whichever answer a child receives, he is unlikely to challenge it—although, knowing children, that question may be followed by a dozen more! As we grow older, however, we ask various forms of that original question in ever-increasing complexity. And we come to insist on fuller answers and the supporting evidence for them. We want both answers and reasonable justifications.

Suppose you are walking in a forest and come to a clearing. There is a tent, hot coffee over a fire, and other evidences of human presence. As you look around, however, no one is in view. You call loudly, and no one seems to hear. How would you react?

It is in the nature of human consciousness to assume that the site belongs to another person who has been present before you. You might choose to look around to find the person or persons who established the camp—especially if there were any abnormal signs of disturbance. You could decide to wait around for a while to see who returns to the site. Or you might simply go on your way. But it would *not* occur to you to say: "Well, fancy this! What a stroke of luck that I came upon a site so perfectly suited to my needs!"

I dare say that you would not walk in, treat the camp as if it were your own, and never entertain the possibility that you were intruding upon another's site. When we see such things, we don't assume that campsites just occasionally occur this way. We know they are set up by someone.

By investigating the site, looking at clothing in the tent, counting the number of cups near the fire, and seeing footprints, you might even have a good idea about the number of persons, their sex, whether adults or children, and why they are in the woods. For example, the coffee, clothing, and footprints might tell you the campers are adults rather than Boy Scouts. The number of chairs and cots might suggest there are three people in the group. The clothing could lead you to believe it is an all-male party, and the equip-

ment might prompt the conclusion that they are on a hunt-
ing trip. You might misinterpret some of the evidence, and
some of your conclusions might have to be refined when
more information surfaces.

The point of the camp illustration is simply that *human
minds look for explanations of phenomena*. We know campsites
don't spring up from nothing. We just will not accept an
it's-just-that-way answer about tents, hot coffee, and rifles
in the woods.

In a similar way, we humans have come upon a clearing
in the cosmos. Planet Earth is here and habitable. "It's just
that way" might seem a sufficient explanation initially. But
the more we think about it, the more we know that this is
no explanation at all. So we begin looking around for clues
that might offer us a reasonable account of why the clearing is here and why it has its particular form. In fact, we
think about our own presence in the clearing as something
else in need of explanation.

Philosophical reasoning about causality (or the lack there-
of), design (or its simulation), and God (or his absence)
stems from the call to investigation that each of us has felt
at coming upon an unexpected state of affairs. Having
stumbled onto a habitable clearing in the cosmic forest, it is
reasonable to ask how things came to be this way. It is both
natural and necessary.

There are only two answers that can be offered with any
plausibility. Either it was created by someone (or something) that existed prior to it and had power and intelligence to bring it into existence *or* it exists quite by chance,
is somehow eternal in nature, and has produced its present
state of order by virtue of natural law.[1]

These two possible answers are stated in representative
fashion in the opening sentences of two books that
approach the subject of origins from contradictory commitments:

"In the beginning God created the heavens and the
earth."[2]

"The Cosmos is all that is or ever was or ever will be."[3]

Our task in this chapter will be to explore the plausibility of these exhaustive and contradictory positions. My confident expectation is to demonstrate that the Eternal God *vs.* Eternal Cosmos choice is settled clearly in favor of the former.

Supernatural Origin vs. Natural Origin

Could our world have originated without an external cause? Is it reasonable to attribute eternality to matter? Could something (the cosmos) have come from nothing?

The existence of Planet Earth as a "habitable clearing in the cosmic forest" (a place fit to be the home of living things) depends on certain very specific features that could not have arranged themselves in the proper relationships to one another. Furthermore, whatever plausibility the theory of evolution gives to the notion that living things are capable of infinite assemblies of properties because of the adaptability of organisms cannot be appealed to here, for the features in mind at this point are those of the nonliving world.[4] Even if we grant that living things can adapt in order to survive, it cannot be granted that nonliving phenomena have any such power. Is Earth simply a series of "miraculous coincidences"?

The term *miraculous coincidences* used above is borrowed from the cover of P. C. W. Davies's book *The Accidental Universe*. Davies is a physicist who has no place in his system for divine causation of the universe. His approach to the subject is typical of an antitheistic prejudice, which presupposes the inadmissibility of God and opts instead for a theory of causation that astounds (and offends) common sense.

Professor Davies speaks over and over again of mysterious constants that are "crucially relevant to the structure of the universe" and "oblige us to accept that the expanding universe has been set up in its motion with a cooperation of astonishing precision."[5] He admits that in studying the general structure of the universe, we encounter "cosmic cooperation of such a wildly improbable nature, it becomes hard to resist the impression that some basic principle is at work."[6] He does not blink to say that "our world is indeed extremely unlikely on *a priori* grounds."[7]

Although Davies will not allow that these things are anything more than "surprisingly fortuitous accidents without which our existence would be impossible,"[8] he offers a long list of fascinating facts that are mind-boggling. For example, if our universe had not expanded at just the right rate, life would not have been possible. If the expansion rate of the nontheist's "big bang" or the theist's "moment of creation" had been slower by a factor of one in a million, the universe would have collapsed before temperatures fell under 10,000 degrees. But if the expansion rate had been greater by the same factor of one in a million, the velocity would have been too much to allow condensation into clumps. Thus, no galaxies would have appeared.

If electrical forces in our cosmos were other than they are, there could be no life. Stronger electrical forces would permit the formation of no element heavier than hydrogen, for the stronger nuclear forces would be unable to overcome proton repulsion. Slightly weaker electrical forces would cause protons to combine too readily, and the sun would explode like a huge thermonuclear bomb.

If nuclear forces were only slightly stronger than they are, life could not have arisen in the universe. The ratio between strong and weak nuclear forces must be as it is. Otherwise, hydrogen nuclei would combine too quickly and turn into helium, or the reaction would not take place at all.

At a less technical level, high school science books point to phenomena of the same sort in abundance. The Earth is tilted at an angle of 23 degrees on its axis and is some 93 million miles from the sun and about 240,000 miles from the moon. If our planet home were not tilted on its axis, water vapor from the oceans would go to the two poles, condense, and pile up as mountains of ice. If Earth rotated

significantly slower than it does at this distance from the
sun, it would not withstand the temperature extremes on
its surface. If the moon were only one-fifth its present distance from Earth, ocean tides would sweep over the tops of
our highest mountains.

Planet Earth has a rich supply of carbon, oxygen, nitro-
gen, and hydrogen—all of which, except hydrogen, appear
to be in short supply elsewhere in the universe and all of
which are essential to life. Four-fifths of its surface is cov-
ered with water, which not only evaporates to give us rain
but also functions to regulate the temperature of the planet. On and on the listing of items of our "fortunate planet"
could go.

Our cosmic home really does appear to be of unique
character. It is consistently within the narrow parameters
of possibility that allow life, as we know it, to exist.
Likening the choice of Planet Earth as a repository for life
to the blindfolded sticking of a pin into a map of the universe, Davies observes:

> Many people of a religious persuasion will no doubt find
> support from these ideas for the belief that the Creator did
> *not* aim the cosmic pin at random, but did so with finely
> computed precision, with the express purpose of selecting a
> universe that *would* be suitable for habitation.[9]

In a paper that acknowledges the "many accidents of
physics and astronomy" that have been necessary to make
our planet habitable, two scientists, James Lovelock and
Sidney Epton, deny God his rightful place as Creator by
offering the "solution" that the Earth itself should be
viewed as divine and responsible for its own intricate balance:

> Life exists only because material conditions on Earth hap-
> pen to be just right for its existence. . . . This view implies
> that life has stood poised like a needle on its point for over
> 3,500 million years. If the temperature or humidity or salin-
> ity or acidity or any one of a number of other variables had

strayed outside a narrow range of values for any length of time, life would have been annihilated.[10]

The authors assign the name of a Greek earth-goddess (Gaia) to our planet and posit the Earth as a living being with the ability to maintain herself in a just-right condition. Surely this is mere metaphor being offered by the writers. If not, it is simply pantheism in new robes. In either case, it is amazing that the alternative of an intelligent planet is preferred by these writers over the more natural possibility of an intelligent Creator-God.

F. R. Tennant was one of the first philosophers of this century to point to these evidences of design in nonliving things as a powerful evidence for eternal involvement in the process by a Creator.[11] Things of the sort he had in mind are the ones already referred to in this chapter in the quotation from Davies or in the article cited by Lovelock and Epton.

Even if the laws of nature and the mechanism of natural selection were held to account adequately for the emergence of *living* things to their present varied and complex states, Tennant argues that the impressive design apparent in *nonliving* things must still be found in an external source of intelligent design. For example, it occurs to us

> . . . that adaptation in inorganic Nature, where there cannot be a formative principle such as nonintelligent organisms evince, should more unequivocally bespeak external design. . . . The fitness of our world to be the home of living beings depends upon certain primary conditions, astronomical, thermal, chemical, etc., and on the coincidence of qualities apparently not causally connected with one another, the number of which would doubtless surprise anyone wholly unlearned in the sciences; and these primary conditions, in their turn, involve many of secondary order.[12]

Tennant refers to this phenomenon as "cosmic teleology" and signifies by the term the whole host of antecedent factors that had to exist in order for life of any form to exist on

Planet Earth. "Presumably the world is comparable with a single throw of dice," he says. "And common sense is not foolish in suspecting the dice to have been loaded."[13]

We understand better now than ever before that "the universe is an unexpectedly hospitable place for living creatures to make their home in."[14]

As to the cavalier attitude of some nontheists that holds that our "lucky planet" is simply at a point where its potential for supporting life is where that of any number of other similar planets like ours has been, is, or one day will be, Fred Hoyle seems to speak the sentiment of a growing number of scientists when he says: "This argument is the veriest nonsense, and if it is to be imbibed at all it must be swallowed with a jorum of strong ale."[15]

The vast universe we inhabit has all the earmarks of having been conceived and arranged according to an intelligent plan rather than by random chance. Everywhere we look in the universe, we see an orderliness about things that invites man to understand his environment through scientific pursuits. Is it reasonable to assign this order to chance? The human mind just doesn't operate that way.

Lest someone should reply that I am already begging the question by referring to instances of apparent design in the universe, allow me to cite a few individuals who are not defenders of theism but who nevertheless concede this point. F. J. Dyson, writing in *Scientific American*, said this about our habitable cosmos: "As we look out into the universe and identify the many accidents of physics and astronomy that have worked together to our benefit, it almost seems as if the universe must in some sense have known we were coming."[16]

Suppose I were to show you a complex computer. We marvel at the sophisticated circuitry, watch in awe as it does complicated mathematical calculations that would otherwise take hours or days, and wag our heads in disbelief as it analyzes data and prints out useful forms of it at lightning speed. Then, after our detailed examination of the machine, suppose I turned to you and said, "Nobody planned or made this computer. It is the chance result of a 'lucky accident,' occurring when a storm blew through a junkyard the other day." You would know immediately that I was either joking with you or totally insane.

As ridiculous as such a fictitious episode sounds, it is more reasonable than the hypothesis that our universe and the life within it, especially the morally sensitive human beings, "just happened." A computer without a manufacturer would be but a minor marvel when compared to a universe without a Creator.

A block of marble does not yield a piece of brilliant sculpture until the hand of a craftsman comes to it. Left to itself, the marble would never make anything of itself. A cosmos filled with nonpurposive and nonintelligent matter would never make itself into a livable environment and place purposive and intelligent human beings within itself. It takes the hand of an all-powerful and infinitely wise Craftsman to bring about such an end.

Denying the Obvious

The *a priori* chance of our universe being such that life will arise in it appears to be one over infinity. In fact, it is easy to imagine an infinite series of universes in which life could not emerge or survive, which equals zero. Since life does exist here, however, the odds must be other than zero. If, following the lead of Professor Davies, we are unwilling to entertain the possibility of a transcendent power to explain it, some other explanation must be offered. For him, it is an infinite number of possible universes.

According to this viewpoint, the very special features of the universe are no longer to be regarded as extraordinary or remarkable, but inevitable. Their apparent improbability is purely a reflection of their unrepresentative nature. The overwhelming majority of universes do not enjoy the conditions consistent with life. Only those rare ones that do are observed.

... Such a universe ... expands from an initially singular condition to a maximum volume, and then collapses back to total obliteration as a final spacetime singularity. ...

The formerly collapsing universe thus 'bounces' out again, revitalized, into a new cycle of expansion and contraction, to be followed by yet another, and so on, *ad infinitum*. In each cycle the structure of the universe is different. If the reprocessing is performed at random, then eventually, purely by chance, the numbers and organization will concur felicitously and the various numerical relations will appear. These cycles will permit the development of cosmologists, who will write books about the extraordinary degree to which nature has conspired to arrange its affairs for the benefit of living beings.[17]

One gets the feeling that a determined (and prejudiced) attempt is being made here to avoid the obvious. Is not the idea of a creative deity a far simpler hypothesis than that of an infinite number of universes? And does the scientific method not urge one to give preference to the simpler of two hypotheses?

The Oscillating Universe Hypothesis, as this notion of the universe alternately expanding and collapsing on itself is often called, is nothing novel to science. It is a highly problematic conjecture, which is inconsistent with the best interpretations we can make of the world external to us. For one thing, the critical density of matter is apparently not great enough to reverse the present expansion of the universe. Robert Jastrow, a respected astronomer who is an agnostic, writes:

A calculation shows that the present expansion of the Universe will be halted if the average density of matter in the Universe corresponds to at least one hydrogen atom in a volume of 10 cubic feet.

How does this threshold value of the density compare with the observed density of matter in the Universe? The matter whose density can be most readily estimated is that which is present in the galaxies in a visible form, as lumi-

nous stars and dense concentrations of gas. If we were to
smear out the visible matter in the galaxies into a uniform
distribution filling the entire Universe, the density of this
smeared-out distribution of matter would be too small by a
factor of 1000 to halt the expansion. . . .

Thus, the facts indicate that the Universe will expand
forever. We still come across pieces of mass here and there
in the Universe, and someday we may find the missing
matter, but the consensus at the moment is that it will not
be found.[18]

Furthermore, the Second Law of Thermodynamics counts
as a weighty piece of evidence against such a theory. The
bottom line of this law is that the universe is becoming
more and more disordered every day. The total disorder
(called "entropy") in any physical system never decreas-
es.[19] Since the universe has a finite amount of order and is
constantly and irreversibly moving from an ordered system to a disordered one, it follows that it cannot have existed forever and that it will eventually perish from what
physicists call "heat death" (the situation of thermo-
dynamic equilibrium where entropy cannot increase).

The opinion of modern science is stated summarily and
concisely by S. A. Bludman of the department of physics of
the University of Pennsylvania:

We now appreciate that, because of the huge entropy generated in our Universe, far from oscillating, a closed universe can only go through one cycle of expansion and
contraction. Whether closed or open, reversing or mono-
tonically expanding, the severely irreversible phase transi-
tions transpiring give the Universe a definite beginning,
middle and end.[20]

Our ordered cosmos did not pop out of nothingness.
Matter is not eternal. Its origination and ordering could not
have been generated by natural causes. Therefore, no one
need ever feel intellectually backward in proposing that it

is reasonable to believe that the existence and character of our universe is due to the creative work of a transcendent power who brought order out of chaos and willed that there should be life.

Whose Explanation Is Better?

The late Bertrand Russell, a determined opponent of Christian theism, confesses that he was rather impressed by a version of the argument just traced until about the age of eighteen. He explains what happened then:

> . . . I read John Stuart Mill's Autobiography, and I there found this sentence: "My father taught me that the question 'Who made me?' cannot be answered, since it immediately suggests the further question 'Who made God?' " That very simple sentence showed me, as I still think, the fallacy in the argument of the First Cause. If everything must have a cause, then God must have a cause. *If there can be anything without a cause, it may just as well be the world as God,* so that there cannot be any validity in that argument [italics added].[21]

This is an instance of what I earlier called "antitheistic prejudice." The very language of the line quoted by Russell, and by which he was so impressed, suggests that it is natural to answer "Who made me?" with a theistic response. Determined to avoid that answer, however, one may argue that an uncaused cosmos is as acceptable as an uncaused deity.

Professor Davies, already cited in this chapter, argues for the same alternative. He posits the origin of the Big Bang as a *"singularity."* This phenomenon is supposed to represent the situation, some 10 to 20 billion years ago, when the total mass of the universe was packed into a single, infinitely dense point. I presume the singularity is supposed to avoid the conundrum created by thinking of non-purposive activity in a "state of nothingness." On the other hand, I can only suppose—since Davies will not allow a deity into his picture—that the singularity had to arise spontaneously from nothing. He writes:

> According to our best scientific understanding of the primeval universe it does indeed seem as though the universe began in the simplest state of all—thermodynamic equilibrium—and that the currently-observed complex structures and elaborate activity only appeared subsequently. It might then be argued that the primeval universe is, in fact, the simplest thing that we can imagine. Moreover, if the prediction of an initial singularity is taken at face value, the universe began in a state of infinite temperature, infinite density and infinite energy. *Is this not at least as plausible as an infinite mind?* [italics added][22]

Unwilling to accept either an eternal universe or an eternal God as Creator—since that choice would lead to the "forbidden" conclusion of God's existence by virtue of matter's noneternal nature—Russell and Davies take what appears to be a *prima facie* irrational posture in opting for a universe that came into being from nothing, while being acted upon by nothing or no one.

Both Russell and Davies conclude with essentially the same punch line: an uncaused universe is just as reasonable as an uncaused God. But is that so? Is an uncaused material world as adequate an explanation of origins as an uncaused personal Creator? I think not.

The latter explanation is far more plausible than the former. A personal Creator God, acting to bring something out of nothing by unlimited wisdom and power, has both logical and practical appeal. The conjecture that the universe was "created spontaneously from nothing *(ex nihilo)*, as a result of established principles of physics" and "had its physical origin as a quantum fluctuation of some pre-existing true vacuum, or state of nothingness"[23] can never generate much excitement for a critical thinker. Our innate rationality is much better satisfied by the presence of God to bring about creation than by the creative powers of a "state of nothingness."

The competing ideas of (a) a universe popping into existence out of nothing (or, for that matter, an eternal universe recycling itself), and (b) an eternal, creative, personal God are *not* equal as stopping points for the set of *Why?* questions that come to us about the cosmos.[24]

Epistemologically, the two terminus points certainly do not have equal adequacy. Given a physical universe (whether eternal or "popping" into place), it remains "logically possible to ask whether it exists in dependence upon the will of a God who is the creator of everything that exists other than himself."[25] On the other hand, the question does not admit of being asked whether such a Being depends on the physical universe, "for his relationship to anything that exists, other than himself, has been defined asymmetrically as that creator to creature."[26] It follows, then, that God and the cosmos are not equally plausible as stopping points for asking Why? about the origin of all material things known to us.

Psychologically, the two terminus points are similarly unequal in explanatory value. David Hume referred to those beliefs or assumptions that are natural to the normally functioning mind as "natural beliefs." If there are such beliefs, surely one of them would be "the tendency of the human mind to find an explanatory finality in conscious acts of will which it does not find in the states of movements of unconscious matter."[27] This tendency traces to our own experiences of free will. "Where did this beautiful painting come from?" is better answered by "Charlotte painted it" than by a discussion of the physics of color and the chemical composition of paints. I have no hesitancy in saying that "In the beginning God created the heavens and the earth" is a better answer to "Whence this cosmos?" than "Our universe is simply one of those things that happens from time to time."

One astronomer, who remains an agnostic in his personal beliefs, has been candid enough to admit the force of the theistic position in light of the cosmological argument:

> Consider the enormity of the problem. Science has proven that the Universe exploded into being at a certain moment. It asks, What causes produced this effect? Who or what put the matter and energy into the Universe? Was the Universe created out of nothing or was it gathered together out of pre-existing materials? And science cannot answer these questions, because, according to the astronomers, in the first moments of its existence the Universe was compressed to an extraordinary degree, and consumed by the heat of a fire beyond human imagination. . . .
>
> Now we would like to pursue that inquiry farther back in time, but the barrier to further progress seems insurmountable. It is not a matter of another year, another decade of work, another measurement or another theory; at this moment it seems as though science will never be able to raise the curtain on the mystery of creation. For the scientist who has lived by faith in the power of reason, the story ends like a bad dream. He has scaled the mountains of ignorance; he is about to conquer the highest peak; as he pulls himself over the final rock, he is greeted by a band of theologians who have been sitting there for centuries.[28]

Personal vs. Impersonal

At this point in formulating a theistic argument, I have heard people say: "The effect of such an argument, even if sound, would not show that God is personal or capable of entering into relationships with people, such as the Bible describes." But there is more to the argument than has been presented to this point.

Some of the more impressive proofs of the existence of a personal deity present themselves to us in startling and paradoxical ways. Consider the case of a man later identified as Arlen D. Williams, Jr., and posthumously presented the Coast Guard's Gold Lifesaving Medal by President Ronald Reagan.

On January 13, 1982, a terrible tragedy occurred in our

nation's capital. Air Florida's Flight 90 crashed shortly after takeoff from Washington's National Airport. Failing to gain necessary altitude, the big jet clipped a bridge over the Potomac River, killing several persons on the bridge, and then toppled into the icy waters, carrying many other helpless people to their deaths. At first glance, such an episode seems to represent a particular instance of the problem of evil (a challenge to theism to be discussed in chapter 4). Upon closer inspection, however, one element of that tragic scene appears to outweigh every other in magnitude. That bright spot amidst tragedy testifies to the fact that man is the creature of a personal and caring God.

In the rescue effort following the crash of Flight 90, six survivors were clinging to the plane's floating tail section. A park police helicopter team hovered above and lowered a lifeline and flotation ring. Each time they lowered it to Mr. Williams, identified at the time in the press only as "the man in the water," and he would pass it on to someone else. He was described by the rescue team as alert and in control. But he was willing to risk being in the icy waters longer for the sake of allowing someone else to be saved.

When the lifeline and flotation ring had been passed to all the others by this brave man, the helicopter team went back to bring him to safety. When they reached the scene, he was gone. The cold water had taken its final casualty that day. As an essay in *Time* magazine put it:

> At some moment in the water he must have realized that he would not live if he continued to hand over the rope and ring to others. He *had* to know it, no matter how gradual the effect of the cold. In his judgment he had no choice. When the helicopter took off with what was to be the last survivor, he watched everything in the world move away from him, and he deliberately let it happen.[29]

Why do human beings have such a capacity within them? If, as some think, man is simply a creature of nature, do you really think such selflessness would be possible? According to the nontheistic view, the instinct for survival is the most fundamental feature of the species. But that heroic man in the water proves that we are *more* than creatures of nature. We are God's creatures and made in his image.

Nature makes no distinctions between good and evil; we humans do. Nature at its best is atoms, molecules, and tissue; humanity at its best is compassion, selflessness, and love. There is something in men and women that is higher and greater than anything nature can produce on its own. Like mere animals, we have instinctive drives. Unlike mere animals, we have a *moral capacity* to judge, restrain, or even overrule our instincts for the sake of some higher duty we sense.

In nature a fountain cannot rise higher than its source. That man has a sense of moral responsibility proves that his origin must be traced to a personal and moral source. That is to say, we must trace our origin not to a struggle for survival and survival of the fittest but to Almighty God. We are hopelessly naive if we witness in others, or experience within ourselves, the moral sensitivities that make us truly human and yet fail to acknowledge God as the only possible explanation that could account for the phenomenon.

As surely as the heavens declare the glory of God, moral human beings declare something of the very likeness to him that is stamped upon our souls. A cosmos filled with nonpurposive and nonintelligent matter would never make itself into a livable environment and place purposive and intelligent human beings within itself. It takes the hand of an all-powerful and infinitely wise deity to turn matter into humanity.

Is it really so hard to believe in God? Or does the *real* difficulty lie in *not* believing?

What, then, does reason tell us about the ultimate explanation of our cosmos? It tells us that a contingent universe cannot be viewed as both cause and effect unto itself, for *ex nihilo nihil fit* ("from nothing comes nothing"). A contingent universe must be explained in terms of a noncontingent (necessary) being who is eternal, self-sufficient, and nonmaterial in nature.

These three qualities—eternality, self-sufficiency, nonmateriality—are immediately apparent about God. That he is *eternal* follows from the self-evident truth that if there had ever been a time when he did not exist, then nothing at all of a contingent nature could ever exist. That he is *self-sufficient* follows definitionally from his identification as a noncontingent necessary being. That he is *nonmaterial* is merely a corollary to his noncontingency, for if God were material in nature, he would automatically become contingent and subject to change.

Reason also tells us that the ultimate explanation for our universe is *infinite in power*. Whether one considers the effect in terms of the vastness of the universe or the power inherent in the fission of an atom, one is rationally forced to admit that the originator of such a creation is omnipotent rather than finite in power.

The source of our cosmos is also obviously *infinite in intelligence*. Brute power, even infinite brute power, could not have created the things we know. Power adequate to create would have to have been directed by an omniscient mind. The intelligence of that mind must have been all-encompassing, so as to have known the future as well as the present, for all the things brought into being were so ordered as to accommodate the totality of life that has been brought into the world from that point of beginning.

Reason also proclaims the *moral nature* of the Creator. The human creatures who inhabit the universe have moral sensitivity. We call some things "good" and others "evil"; we judge some actions to be praiseworthy and others blameworthy. This moral sense cannot have come to us from a source that is amoral.

Does anyone ask how we could be justified in inferring the *personal nature* of God from this argument? If the argument presented here proves anything at all, it proves that the God discovered at its conclusion could not be spoken of as mere Cosmic Mind or Impersonal Force. Creative power, intelligence, and morality are the very ingredients of personality.

The ultimate "explanation" of this cosmos is an eternal, self-sufficient, nonmaterial, infinitely powerful, infinitely wise, and moral *person*. Definitionally, there can be only one level at which infinite personal attributes exist. Thus, God is one, a unity rather than many. Practically, we see the evidence throughout the cosmos of a *uni*-verse of order rather than a *multi*-verse of disorder.

Such a being is obviously no "God of the gaps" who functions for superstitious people as an explanation to cover the holes in their ignorance. As surely as there are gaps and holes in our knowledge of the *secondary causes* that work within nature (the behavior of subatomic particles), an enlightened theist has never invoked the name of God to fill them. The name *God* is reserved for the identification of the *Ultimate Cause* lying behind all other causal agents and powers. As a Christian, for example, I understand much of the scientific explanation of the secondary causes related to conception and childbirth; at the birth of my children, however, I gave thanks to God as the primary cause of life in general and their lives in particular. The concern of this chapter has been not with proximate and immediate causes, which science is legitimately concerned to pursue, but with the cause to which every contingent being ultimately traces its origin.

I do not claim to have set forth a proof of God's existence that cannot be challenged, or one that sweeps away the possibility of counter-argument. The two primary challenges that can be made to the case presented here will be considered at some length in the two chapters immediately following.

My claim is more modest. I claim to have shown in the first two chapters of this book: (1) that belief in unseen things is not irrational; (2) that one who can believe in the truth and practicality of modern quantum physics (staggering as its concepts are) ought not to see an initial impossibility in believing in God by virtue of its staggering implications; (3) that our obligation with regard to our beliefs is careful reasoning based on observed data; and (4) that careful reasoning concerning the nature of the cosmos we inhabit constitutes a legitimate base for faith in the God of Christian theism.

Conclusion

Where did the creative power come from—that which was necessary to bring this universe into being? The hard facts point beyond natural causes to a supernatural cause. *Reason points to God.*

After delivering a lecture on the solar system, a speaker was approached by an elderly lady who claimed she had an explanation better than his. "We don't live on a ball revolving around the sun," she said. "We live on a crust of earth on the back of a giant turtle."

The speaker attempted to deal with his critic gently. He asked, "If your theory is correct, madam, what does the turtle stand on?"

"You're a clever man, and that is a good question. But I can answer it. The first turtle stands on the back of a second, far-larger turtle."

"But what does this second turtle stand on?" he asked patiently.

The old woman smiled triumphantly. "It's no use," she announced. "It's turtles all the way down."

In a delightfully funny way, this story sums up the total set of questions discussed in this chapter. Since every thing and every event in the physical universe depends for its explanation on something outside itself, we are forced to choose between either physical events causing physical events to infinity—or God. We do not have the options of nonintelligent, nonpersonal matter acting on itself to create intelligent, personal beings or God. The former options are not answers at all, for they merely defer the answer for the cause of one event, by appealing to another event which is equally unable to explain itself. Apart from God, it is turtles without an end!

When thoughtful people look at the nature of our cosmos and reflect on their own self-consciousness about moral issues, they are examining the fingerprints that God has left on his creation. "For since the creation of the world God's invisible qualities—his eternal power and divine nature—have been clearly seen, being understood from what has been made, so that men are without excuse" (Rom. 1:20).

3

Whose Creature Is Man?

"But by far the most potent single factor to undermine popular belief in the existence of God in modern times," suggests Colin Brown, "is the evolutionary theory of Charles Darwin."[1]

At the level of intellectual discussion, Brown is probably correct. People who believed in a "God of the gaps" were dealt a severe blow as modern science filled so many of the gaps in human knowledge during the last century or so. Even some apologists for Christian faith whose notion of causality was too limited by virtue of inadequate philosophic or scientific training felt that something crucial had been lost to the advance of science.

Has life come from natural selection, genetic mutation, and other natural phenomena rather than from a Supreme Being? Has evolution moved God from center stage and taken the spotlight? If one chooses to hold to a theistic belief, is he now obliged to adapt his concept of deity to the evolutionary creed?

Two Levels of Causality

It is certainly possible that the Ultimate Cause of the universe could have employed evolution as a *secondary cause* within his creative scheme. There is no defensible *a priori* reason for seeing God and evolution as incompatible concepts. Whether they are, in fact, compatible would have to be determined by something other than human testimony—for there were no human witnesses to the origin of the cosmos or the life within it.

In fact, if the theory of evolution were capable of being proved factually true beyond a shadow of doubt, nothing about the argument for God's existence presented in chapter 2 of this book would be destroyed or even jeopardized in any fundamental way. If causality is understood in terms of ultimate explanatory adequacy, the theistic explanation for the existence of our universe wins hands down over its materialistic alternative. The existence of an eternal, self-sufficient, and creative deity is a uniquely ultimate fact in a way that a physical universe's existence could never be.

In simple terms, if one found that the intricate computer of our previous chapter owed its origin not to an intelligent designer but to an automated, self-monitoring factory without a single person inside its doors, a rational mind would then ask *who* (not *what*) designed such an ingenious factory. If anything, a self-generating, self-repairing factory would be more marvelous than the computers it generated. So if this cosmos were shown to function and produce intelligent beings through self-monitoring biologic processes (evolution), the minds of people observing it would naturally think of the possible explanations for its origin and think back to God in the same way we did in the previous chapter.

If the general theory of evolution—as opposed to the *micro*-evolutionary change which both theists and nontheists admit—were somehow capable of being proved true, it is not the existence of God that would be called into question but the accuracy of the Bible as an alleged account of the origin of human life. Such an event would also seem to have the significance of calling into question the deity of Jesus Christ, for he clearly accepted the biblical account of creation as true—an indictment, if he were wrong, of the supernatural wisdom we would expect from God in the flesh.

Since this book has already tipped its author's hand as one committed to the total truthfulness of the Christian religion, a reader would not expect capitulation on this point. Indeed, although evolution would not jeopardize the theistic argument presented in the preceding chapter, I happen to think that it is a mistaken theory. Furthermore, especially in view of the conflict in the popular mindset between theism and evolution, some space needs to be given to an explanation of the theory of evolution and its larger relationship to the whole apologetic enterprise.

This chapter will show that the general theory of organic evolution neither replaces God as the ultimate explainer for the things we experience in the world nor jeopardizes the anticipated possibilities of making credible cases for the inspiration of Scripture and the deity of Jesus Christ.

Some Preliminary Matters

The initial task of this chapter is to get clear in our minds what the theory of evolution offers as an interpretive model. Only then can we sort out things that agree with or challenge a theistic interpretive model (some form of divine creation) and begin to weigh some of the relevant evidence. Since much dogmatism and mud-slinging have gotten into discussions of this topic in the past, we would do well to avoid that sort of thing in any serious investigation of important issues.

Sometimes it is the theist-creationist who tries to poison the well against his opponent by labeling evolutionists "godless," "anti-Christian," "immoral," and so forth. The sort of publicity generated by Scopes-type trials is a case in point of the type of thing that makes serious apologists cringe.

One of the pro-creationism witnesses in a 1981 Arkansas trial testified about his confidence that supernatural creation is scientific, harmonizes with all we know about living things, and deserves to be presented in biology texts and public school classes. Under cross-examination, he also expressed his confidence that aliens have visited Planet Earth via spaceships and that such visits are associated with demonic forces. He immediately became a model caricature of "anti-intellectual creationists." It was a status entirely deserved. In light of multiple episodes of this sort, does anyone wonder why evolution has gained widespread acceptance as the view of rational thinkers and creationism is increasingly regarded as superstition?

If the evidence falsifies a creationist view of origins, one may still hold the view as a matter of blind credulity. (For example, there is a Flat Earth Society headquartered in Great Britain.) One cannot, however, claim to have *rational* faith in it, for rational faith must rest on evidence and proofs and may never defy them. Both evolution and creation are *philosophic interpretations of data* from the natural sciences. Both are interpretive models rather than secrets read off the data. Thus, it is the philosophy of science rather than biology or theology that must judge the method, theories, and results of such issues.

On the other hand, it is sometimes the evolutionist who is pejorative, unfair, and guilty of inexcusable misrepresentation. Take as an example of this sort of thing the introduction to an article by Isaac Asimov:

> Scientists thought it was settled.
> The universe, they had decided, is about 20 billion years old, and Earth itself is 4.5 billion years old. Simple forms of life came into being more than three billion years ago, having formed spontaneously from nonliving matter. They grew more complex through slow evolutionary processes and the first hominid ancestors of humanity appeared more than four million years ago. Homo sapiens itself—the present human species, people like you and me—has walked the earth for at least 50,000 years.
> But apparently it isn't settled. There are Americans who believe that the earth is only about 6,000 years old; that human beings and all other species were brought into exis-

tence by a divine Creator as eternally separate varieties of beings, and that there has been no evolutionary process.[2]

Here Dr. Asimov not only slides over such issues as spontaneous generation of life from nonliving matter as if they were trivial but also assigns three positions to creationists that are *not* held by responsible apologists. Few would argue that the earth is "only about 6,000 years old," that all the presently known species of living things were brought into being simultaneously at the initial creation, or that there has been "no evolutionary process" at work in the past or observable at present among living things.

At the start of this chapter, then, permit me to state my personal views on a whole range of issues involved in the so-called creation-evolution debate.

1. Both evolution and creation are interpretive models for the data provided by science. Neither model is capable of being established by the scientific method of observation and repeatability.

2. Each model has strengths and weaknesses. Neither is immune to criticism from the other.

3. During an earlier time of religious dogmatism, the scientific community was unjustly shackled in its pursuit of truth by prejudice, which attacked the character and intelligence of those who proposed the evolutionary model for serious investigation. Today, the shoe is on the other foot, and the dogmatism of antisupernaturalism is sometimes seen in the attacks made against divine creation and the intimidation of both young and old from voicing their honest convictions.

4. Pejorative language and mud-slinging are out of place in serious discussions among honest people. Creationists are unjustified in slurring (if not slandering) their opponents' morality or honesty. Evolutionists are equally wrong in resorting to *ad hominem* arguments that characterize all who defend supernatural creation as "anti-intellectual," "ignorant," "scientifically illiterate," and so forth. Neither side in this long-standing debate is free of guilt in fudging

the data, evading difficulties, and misrepresenting the opposite view.

I repeat: *Both evolution and creation are philosophic interpretations of data from the natural sciences.* Both are interpretive models rather than secrets read off the data. Neither view is without difficulty. In fact, no position on any subject is free of possible criticisms or hard problems. We will get back to the problems later, but let's begin by getting a handle on the current status of evolutionary theory.

The Debate Among Evolutionists

Modern evolutionary thought traces back to Charles Darwin (1809–1882). In 1859 he published his famous *The Origin of Species.*

As a theory of origins, evolution certainly did not originate with Darwin. Evolutionary accounts of the origin of life date back at least to the Greek period and have vied with creationist accounts from the earliest of times. Nonetheless, serious discussion of modern evolutionary thought characteristically begins with Darwin's work.

Darwin observed the apparent waste in nature when living things (frogs) produce a great number of offspring, only to have a relative few survive to reproduce themselves. By a process he called "natural selection," Darwin theorized that those surviving to reproduce must have had traits making them more likely to survive—the "survival of the fittest." Over generations and generations, he theorized, this process would be expected to yield organisms particularly suited to their environments. Given the variety of environments available on Planet Earth, initially simple structures in plants and animals could become very complex and highly varied over long periods of time.

In essence, then, Darwin held that all species have descended from a small base of primordial ancestors—perhaps only one source, and, at most, a very few sources—by a slow and gradual process dictated by natural selection. As plants and animals competed over limited resources within their environments, the fittest of the species survived and passed on their advantages to future generations. Given enough time, Darwin believed, a significantly large number of changes would have accumulated so that the latest generation would be identifiable as a separate species from its ancestors.

To Darwin, this was not a chance process in the hands of blind luck. The variations and changes within a given group of offspring might be random (pure chance), but the process of natural selection imposed a weeding-out process by favoring those variations that improved the plant or animal's ability to survive and reproduce. With the environment of an organism naturally selecting the occasional changes in its structures that favored its chances for survival, slow transformations from one form of living thing to another occurred (the origin of new species). In Darwin's own words:

> Can it, then, be thought improbable, seeing that variations useful to man have undoubtedly occurred, that other variations useful in some way to each being in the great and complex battle of life, should occur in the course of many successive generations? If such do occur, can we doubt (remembering that many more individuals are born than can possibly survive) that individuals having any advantage, however slight, over others, would have the best chance of surviving and procreating their kind? On the other hand, we may feel sure that any variation in the least degree injurious would be rigidly destroyed.[3]

As to the observability of these processes, Darwin added: "We see nothing of these slow changes in progress, until the hand of time has marked the lapse of ages, and then so imperfect is our view into long-past geological ages, that we see only that the forms of life are now different from what they formerly were."[4]

The major problems with Darwinism were related to fossils and principles of inheritance. Darwin admitted that the fossil record did not support the gradual ascent of living things claimed by his theory. He was confident, however, that the imperfection of the fossil record would be remedied with further research by paleontologists. The gaps would close and the "missing links" would surely be discovered.

Without a knowledge of genetics, Darwin was admittedly puzzled about the issue of inheritance. How did the traits favorable to an organism's survival pass from parents to children? Some concessions appear to be made in *The Origin* to the Lamarckian theory of inheritance of acquired characteristics. For the most part, though, he seems to have thought that natural selection was adequate to explain the phenomenon. Given long, long periods of time, the accumulation of very small advantages to an organism through natural selection was supposed to change things from amoeba to reptile to bird—to man.

The pioneer work of such geneticists as Gregor Mendel and Hugo de Vries put a new wrinkle into evolutionary theory. As the hereditary units (genes) of living organisms began to yield their secrets, we learned that permanent and large-scale modification of a plant or animal could take place through a process called "mutation."

At this point, a heated controversy began to develop between evolutionists who were defensive of Darwinian gradualism and those who chose to place their confidence in genetic mutation as the mechanism for the process. After all, the fossil record still had not yielded the fine-tuning that Darwin had predicted; the missing links were still missing at all the crucial junctures. Perhaps, some suggested, genetic mutation had caused dramatic changes to occur suddenly rather than over long periods of time. As late as the 1960s, however, Darwinian gradualism still had the upper hand in the debate.

Then came Stephen Jay Gould and Niles Eldredge in 1972 and 1977, with the publication of major scientific papers challenging gradualism and championing what they called "punctuated equilibrium." Deeply troubled by the Darwinian theory of gradual evolution and the inconsistencies they believed it generated, they proposed a theory of rapid and infrequent changes of major proportions within a population.

Instead of the slow accumulation of gradual changes, Gould and Eldredge see species enduring with relatively little or no change for very long periods of time. A given organism maintains itself in stable equilibrium. Occasionally, however, that organism's history is punctuated by a rapid outbreak of morphological changes, which result in the establishment of new species. This explains for the punctuationists the absence of transitional forms in the fossil record. In their view of evolution, change occurs so rapidly and infrequently as to preclude the intermediate forms, the missing links that gradualists assume but cannot produce from the paleontological record.

In the model of evolution by punctuated equilibrium, the importance of natural selection is minimized. The emergence of new species is explained by the random internal process of genetic mutation. When a small stock of an organism is somehow isolated from its general population—perhaps by a geological disruption in the environment—it is theorized that a major genetic change could occur whereby new traits would emerge with no particular survival value involved. Within this limited gene pool, inbreeding would occur and quickly stamp the changes as permanent within that group. Thus, the environmental selection process so crucial to Darwin is seen by punctuationists to select whole species rather than isolated individuals.

Gould himself explains the basic character of the theory as follows:

> We proposed the theory of punctuated equilibrium largely to provide a different explanation for pervasive trends in the fossil record. Trends, we argued, cannot be attributed to gradual transformation within lineages, but must arise from the differential success of certain kinds of

species. A trend, we argued, is more like climbing a flight of stairs (punctuations and stasis) than rolling up an inclined plane.[5]

Presently, heated debate is going on between the gradualists and the punctuationists. Each group grants some legitimacy to the other's claims but also pokes large holes in the rival theory that seem incapable of being filled. Punctuationists, for example, point to the fossil record as a major problem with gradualism. Gradualists respond by citing what is known about the harmful rather than beneficial tendencies of genetic mutation and scoffing at the idea that such a negative force could be taken as the driving mechanism behind evolution.

Most evolutionists are neither "pure" gradualists nor "pure" punctuationists, opting for some sort of synthesis between these two views. Others more boldly say that some third alternative (excluding divine creation as that alternative!) must be forthcoming.

False Issues Between Creation and Evolution

There are many points within the evolutionary model to which the theist-creationist takes no exception. Because the battle is sometimes pitched at these points, however, it will be helpful to identify some issues where conflict is not inevitable.

For one thing, informed theists do not deny that some "evolution" occurs among living things. The term is in quotation marks in the statement just made to alert the reader to the need for a precise definition for the word in question.

The word *evolution* fundamentally means nothing more than "change." Of course, change occurs in all living things. New species of peas, flowers, bacteria, dogs, and squirrels have been (and are being) produced—both in nature and under laboratory conditions. The more precise term to use for this sort of change is "microevolution."

Countless varieties and occasional new species are produced by this process.

When the word in question is most commonly used, however, it is designed to refer to a much more comprehensive level of change whereby one can accept that the emergence of birds, for example, is traced back to a particular kind of reptile. This is more technically called "macroevolution" (or, less frequently, megaevolution).

As a special theory, microevolution is unquestionably true and capable of demonstration; as a general theory, macroevolution is far more removed from basic data and therefore incapable of direct testing. Much of the going round in circles between theist-creationists and nontheist-evolutionists is fruitless because of a failure to be clear about what is under discussion. An evolutionist may defend the "theory of evolution" (specific or general?) by means of an abundant supply of data on *micro*evolution and think he has proved *macro*evolution. A theist may challenge the "theory of evolution" (specific or general?) by raising the problems inherent within *macro*evolution and think himself somehow committed to deny *micro*evolution as well.

Species are not fixed and immutable. The biblical category of "kind" is not intended to be a technical term of Linnean classification and certainly does not correspond with the technical use of "species" within that taxonomic system.

Neither are theists committed to a view that requires dishonesty with the fossil record. There are indeed transitional forms (to microevolution) in the fossil record. There are also many life forms in the fossil record that apparently no longer survive on Planet Earth (dinosaurs).

One Bible college instructor with whom I have some acquaintance actually denied in his classes that such creatures as dinosaurs ever existed. When pressed about what paleontologists were digging up and exhibiting in museums of natural science, he replied they were either man-made frauds or satanic deceptions placed there to try to deceive the elect.

The fossil record is real and supports the special theory of microevolution, just as the living record of organisms supports that special theory. The extinct forms of life in the record are of no help to—and often harm—the general theory (macroevolution). They are certainly not transitional in character. In fact, as will be discussed later in this chapter, the glaring absence of clear transitional forms is puzzling, to say the least, for the defender of the general theory.

For another thing, theists are not committed to standing against the witness of geology to insist, with Archbishop Ussher, that the world was created at 9:00 A.M. on October 23, 4004 B.C. One must do strange and irresponsible things not only with science but with Scripture as well to derive the notion of an earth no older than a few thousand years.

Against the claim of some that the cosmos could have been created five seconds ago by an omnipotent God who imbedded all our notions of memory and past experience into our minds, I would protest that such a notion is absurd. A God who pulled such a trick on his creatures would not be moral. He would, instead, be a cruel deceiver and dishonest. Similarly, it seems equally implausible to think that God created only a few thousand years ago a cosmos that has all the earmarks of great age (light from distant stars visible on Planet Earth, the Grand Canyon, etc.) and thereby deceives us.

When the "beginning" of Genesis 1:1 actually was is unknown and unknowable to mortals. Both theists and nontheists agree that human life in its present habitable environment is a relatively recent phenomenon (cf. Asimov's estimate of 50,000 years). The whole problem of dating ancient artifacts calls for more humility than is generally demonstrated by disputants from either group. The radiocarbon dating system developed by Professor Libby dates earth's atmosphere at around 10,000 years.[6] An article in the *Journal of Geophysical Research* documented tremendous errors in the dating of rocks by the potassium-argon method; eight dated samples of volcanic materials with the known formation date of 1800 and 1801 yielded ages ranging from 160 million years to almost three billion years.[7]

Finally, there is the fact that responsible apologists can often agree with critics of theism and divine creation that some proffered interpretations of Scripture defy rational faith and bring the total effort at defending theism into disrepute. The examples already cited concerning Archbishop Ussher and the Bible college instructor are cases in point. One must be careful not to use the Bible to "prove" things it does not presume to speak about. Clearly poetic sections must not be pressed for scientific accuracy by critics or for pre-scientific insights by believers. Honesty with texts as to their nature and purpose must guide their responsible exegesis.

Why Creation Is More Reasonable

The Alternative to a Theistic Account of Life

Nontheistic explanations of life within our universe ultimately reduce to a counter-scientific requirement of *spontaneous generation of life*. This is the process referred to by Asimov in the opening of this chapter. He spoke of simple forms of life "having formed spontaneously from nonliving matter" several billion years ago.

The common postulation from nontheists is that the primary building blocks of life (nucleotides and amino acids) were produced from molecules of water, methane, and ammonia interacting with electricity in the absence of free oxygen. For the sake of argument, we shall not force the issue again just here by prying into the origin of water, methane, ammonia, or matter in general—though the move from "nothing" to "something" is as insurmountable an obstacle for nontheistic theories of origins as the move "from something" to "life."

Laboratory experiments in recent years have concocted an organic "soup" of compounds believed essential to the appearance of the first life. But the decisive step from this primordial brew to the formation of replicating macro-molecules and then to an actual organism, or a primitive cell, is inexplicable.

A Nobel Prize-winning French biochemist who is a thoroughgoing evolutionist refers to these steps as "major difficulties" and acknowledges that the *a priori* probability of their resolution by chance circumstances is "virtually zero." Yet Jacques Monod and others like him assume it must have happened, for *life is here*.[8] That approach to a problem is neither good science nor good logic.

French scientist Louis Pasteur demonstrated to the larger scientific community that life does not arise spontaneously from nonliving material. Before his work, many people believed that worms, for example, were the end product of horse-hairs swelling up in mud and coming to life, that maggots were the by-products of rotting meat, and so forth. Evolutionists must beg the question about spontaneous generation to begin their process. Is supernatural creation by an intelligent and powerful deity an absurd alternative here?

Except as a necessity for getting evolution off the ground, modern science has no room for the theory that living things arise spontaneously from nonliving ones. For the theory of evolution, however, spontaneous generation had to happen. It does not—there is no scientific evidence that it ever has.

Here are two nontheists who say the same thing—and then go on to resist the possibility of divine creation. Could there be a prejudice at work, even among people trained in science's "objective methodology"?

> Yet as biochemists discover more and more about the awesome complexity of life, it is apparent that the chances of it originating by accident are so minute that they can be completely ruled out. Life cannot have arisen by chance.[9]

The problem is that a self-replicating robot has been

designed to build copies of itself, whereas the chemical reactions that led to the first living organism must have happened entirely by chance. Yet the odds against such a chance occurrence seem insuperable—by any statistical standards, plain impossible.[10]

Design in Nature

With respect to the living things that inhabit our globe, the evidences for design are frequent and impressive. As Richard Lewontin of Harvard University puts it, many organisms "appear to have been carefully and artfully designed." That fact is, he says, "the chief evidence of a Supreme Designer."[11]

In the case of plants, animals, or organs, it is important to realize that they have to appear in functional form. Compare the way we have developed such instruments as television, rockets, and the like. It has largely been a system of trial and error. One idea that didn't work became the steppingstone to another and so on. Only at the end of a long and difficult process did we have working devices that were important to us. In living organisms, though, the process is significantly different. There is no time for trial and error. It must work to the creature's advantage from the beginning.

But don't evolutionists argue that the trial-and-error process is exactly what has brought living organisms to their present states? Yes, they argue that until they come under close questioning. Then they begin to fall back a bit and give some ground. By virtue of the principles of natural selection and survival of the fittest, a partially developed structure is a liability and would be rejected rather than tolerated for fine-tuning. In many instances, in fact, partially developed structures would mean the death of the organism.

Francis Hitching, a scientist seeking to find a nontheistic way to explain what he terms "evolutionary novelties" (organs of extreme complexity), admits that such a struc-

ture as the eye either functions as a whole, or not at all. He
writes:

> The eye is, in fact, merely an extreme example of a large
> number of *evolutionary novelties*, as they have come to be
> termed—structures that, logically, have either to be perfect,
> or perfectly useless. . . . Theory demands that successive
> steps of a gradually improving nature build towards a final
> product perfectly adapted to its environment. But many of
> the proposed intermediate steps seem impractical or even
> harmful. What use would be half a jaw? Or half a lung?
> Natural selection would eliminate creatures with such odd-
> ities, not preserve them.
>   Secondly, simultaneous advantageous mutations seem-
> ingly have to take place. Otherwise, the organ, even half-
> formed, would not work at all. In the eye, for instance, the
> pinhole opening (the pupil) and the lens have to work
> together. Statisticians call this a *system of coordinated vari-
> ables*.
>   It is extremely difficult for two variables to function in
> harmony—and in the eye, as we have seen, there are many
> more than two. The problem is coordination. Indeed, calcu-
> lations have been made about the odds against the eye hav-
> ing evolved by chance alone. They turned out to be of an
> astronomical order—at least ten billion to one against, and
> perhaps many orders of magnitude more improbable even
> than that.[12]

One of my favorite examples of a case in nature that is
intelligible in the case of supernatural design and otherwise absurd involves an insect. *Brachinus*, better known as
the bombardier beetle, squirts a lethal mixture of two
chemicals into the face of its enemy. When the two chemicals mix, they explode. In order to store those two chemicals in its own body until needed for self-defense, a
chemical inhibitor is there to make them harmless. At the
instant the beetle squirts the stored liquid from its tail, an
anti-inhibitor is added to make the mixture explosive
again. The slightest alteration in the chemical balance

Whose Creature Is Man?   73

involved here would result in a race of exploded beetles in only one generation. How reasonable is it to put this complex process down to a lucky roll of the dice as opposed to creative design?[13]

> This extraordinary device is a wonderful aid to survival *now that it is perfected.* But if it was produced by the blind trial-and-error method of evolution, what horrors the earlier generations of beetles must have endured for the sake of posterity.
>
> Anybody who has ever worked in a research laboratory will have no difficulty in visualizing a stern-faced Mother Nature, addressing the grief-stricken survivors of one of the earlier, unsuccessful experiments:
>
> "Never mind, lads. It's worth pressing on. This is going to be the ultimate weapon. When we've got it perfected it will make you the masters of the insect world. We shall need to change the formula of Ingredient A, increase the injection rate of B to give more thorough mixing, improve the detonator, and widen the flame orifice to keep the blast pressure down—oh, yes, and we'll thicken up the walls of the combustion chamber to give you more protection. I'm sure we shan't lose so many of you in the next set of trials."
>
> Seriously, though, isn't it obvious that natural forces alone could never have produced a bombardier beetle? Natural selection would very soon have exterminated the first beetles to start playing with fire, long before the beetles' weapons became an aid to survival. Nature would have had to have known where she was going, and to have been determined to get there whatever the cost, when she first started fitting flamethrowers into beetles.
>
> And since nature is not an intelligent being, and consequently has no sense of purpose, there must be Somebody behind nature who designed and built the strange weaponry of the bombardier beetle.[14]

Conclusion

Each person must be left to judge the alternatives of theistic and nontheistic explanations for the origins of our universe and life within it. But the clear weight of reason seems to many of us to come down decisively on the side of the theistic model.

To claim the very least for this chapter, it has shown that nothing about modern science has made the theistic world view either logically or practically untenable. More than that, it has raised several questions that the general theory of evolution, or *macro*evolution, simply cannot answer.

Evolution does *not* remove the role of a creative deity from the cosmos. It is a poor alternative to a more natural interpretation of the data, which sees our world and intelligent life within it as the result of the creative genius and power of God.

4

Suffering and a Loving God

In the previous chapter, the relationship of theism to modern advances in science and the theory of evolution was discussed. That chapter began with the claim that Darwin's theory of evolution has served to undermine popular belief in God at the level of intellectual discussion. In this chapter, we turn to the more practical and personal issue that has challenged faith in a loving and powerful God from the earliest of times: suffering.

No piece of literature raises this issue more vividly than the Bible. Although the character Job was God-fearing, upright, and prosperous, all of a sudden his world tumbled down around him. All ten of his children were killed when a house collapsed on them during a party; he suffered severe financial reverses when his crops were destroyed in the field and his flocks and herds were lost; then he became terribly ill with a disease that caused him intense pain and suffering.

The range of issues associated with this theme of human suffering is customarily summed up as "the problem of evil." In its simplest form, the problem of evil challenges theism with this question: How can the existence of a benevolent and omnipotent God be reconciled with the fact of so much misery in the world he is supposed to have created?

Understanding the Issue

While a theist points to various phenomena in the cosmos that he alleges to be inexplicable *without* the existence of God, a nontheist points to other phenomena that he alleges to be inexplicable *with* the existence of God. Such negative things as animal pain, human suffering, and man's inhumanity to man are held to be incompatible with the existence of a just, merciful, and powerful deity.

Three hundred years before Christ, Epicurus gave this problem its classical philosophic formulation: If God wants to prevent evil but cannot, he is not omnipotent; if he is powerful enough to prevent evil but will not, he is not benevolent; if he neither can nor desires to prevent evil, there is no good reason to think of him as "divine" at all; if he both can and wishes to prevent evil, there is no way to account for its presence in our experience; thus, since evil clearly does exist, we must conclude that no omnipotent and omnibenevolent God exists.

In Part X of his *Dialogues Concerning Natural Religion*, David Hume has one of his central characters, Philo, admit that the evidences of apparent design in nature can be taken to point to God's existence by a rational person. But that force is mitigated, he claims, by the argument from evil:

> Were a stranger to drop, in a sudden, into this world, I would show him as a specimen of its ills, an hospital full of diseases, a prison crowded with malefactors and debtors, a field of battle strowed with carcasses, a fleet floundering in the ocean, a nation languishing under tyranny, famine, or pestilence. To turn the gay side of life to him, and give him a notion of its pleasures; whither should I conduct him? to a ball, to an opera, to court? He might justly think that I was only showing him a diversity of distress and sorrow.
>
> There is no evading such striking instances, said Philo, but by apologies, which still farther aggravate the charge. Why have all men, I ask, in all ages, complained incessantly of the miseries of life?[1]

Hume summarizes his indictment by referring back to the formulation of this problem already cited from Greek philosophy: "Epicurus' old questions are yet unanswered. Is he willing to prevent evil, but not able? then he is impotent. Is he able, but not willing? then he is malevolent. Is he both able and willing? whence then is evil?"[2]

Are the questions of Epicurus unanswered—perhaps even unanswerable? This chapter will face up to them squarely and offer some answers for readers to consider. It will be an exercise in "theodicy" (a defense of God's goodness and power in view of the problem of evil).

Elements of a Successful Theodicy

The first order of business is to identify the elements that must be present in any successful theodicy. There are four items that appear to be necessary:

1. In a successful theodicy, both God's benevolence and power must be defended.

There simply is no problem of evil if one envisions a deity whose character is malevolent or mixed (possessed of good and bad features). Evils within man's environment would be expected to occur if the deity who created him were conceived of as less than wholly good. Within the context of traditional theism, such a being would not be worthy of worship and adoration.

Neither will it do to suggest that the problem of evil issues from a faulty concept of "goodness" on our part. Some have claimed that no standard external to God can be used as the norm of goodness and that we are obligated to praise as "good" anything God chooses to do. This approach holds that infinite goodness is unrelated to the degree of goodness that mortals can comprehend. While it is true that infinite goodness is qualitatively beyond mortal comprehension, the category of things we term "good" must correspond in quality to the finite goodness that mortals experience; otherwise, the very word is meaningless and should not be used.

Also, the problem of evil requires that God be viewed as a being of maximally great (infinite) power. Because the "omnipotence" of God is such a confused topic in the discussion of theodicy, we must take the time to make some clarifications here.

Mackie demonstrates a common error with regard to the Judeo-Christian doctrine of divine omnipotence. He takes the term to mean that "there are no limits to what an omnipotent thing can do."[3] Clearly this definition will not do. Thomas Aquinas long ago insisted that "this phrase, *God can do all things*, is rightly understood to mean that God can do all things that are possible."[4]

Omnipotence is best understood as the ability to do anything that is not self-contradictory or in violation of moral perfection.

To say that the deity is unable to make a rock so big he cannot lift it, an automobile whose dimensions are larger on the inside than the outside, a knife so sharp it can slice bread thinly enough to have only one side, or a round square is not to admit that things have been discovered that God *could* do if he had more power than he presently possesses. All these are impossible things that entail logical self-contradictions. Rather than say that God is deficient in power due to an inability to perform these feats, one need say only that these are things that are not subject to accomplishment.

To say that God cannot act in violation of his own moral perfection is simply to insist that he cannot act contrary to his inherent qualities, which cause him to be good, and to wish all things to be like him insofar as possible.

If someone is ready to object that omnipotence dies the death of a thousand qualifications when defined this way, he should realize that the problem of evil cannot be generated without the two provisions just specified. Unless God is bound to operate within the laws of logic—that is, unable to perform self-contradictory things—he could exist and decree that propositions in contradiction can still be true. In such a case, a theist could admit that the contention of some that "God exists" and "evil exists" are contradictory propositions, yet maintain that God is simply not subject to the laws of logic. Again, unless God is bound to act in harmony with his inherent moral perfection, he could exist and act in ways that are sometimes incompatible with his general goodness.

2. A successful theodicy must acknowledge the reality of moral and natural evils in the world.

Systems ranging from pantheism to Christian Science have chosen to deny the objective reality of evil. Evil is declared to be mere illusion, and both "good" and "evil" become nonsense words. Even the Augustinian approach of calling evil a "privation of that which is good" holds implicitly that evil has no objective existence of its own. If evil is mere illusion or privation, how can one do battle with it or overcome it?

The term *moral evil* signifies everything that is thought of as "sin" within the Judeo-Christian tradition. It is man's rebellion against his Creator, his failure to live by the right standards God has revealed, and his inhumanities to his fellow creatures. War, lying, murder, rape—all these are specific instances of moral evil.

The term *natural evil* signifies a broad range of things lying outside man's culpability that, nevertheless, increase human pain and suffering. It includes physical evils that seem to be involved in the very constitution of the environment in which we live. Parasites, earthquakes, birth defects, diseases—all these are specific instances of natural evil.

3. An adequate response to the problem of evil must offer a rationally acceptable and morally good reason for the existence of natural evil in a world created by a deity of infinite power and benevolence.

The best candidate for such a reason is what Reichenbach has called the "rational exigency that God created according to laws."[5] What does such a claim entail?

God is obliged to work within a medium that is inherently contingent (matter) and therefore limited as to its possibilities (natural laws). A potter works with clay, which has certain qualities: it is malleable, capable of holding impressions, able to be dried and hardened, and so forth. These qualifications both enable and limit the craftsman as he works. Similarly, a creative deity works with a physical world capable of supporting sentient creatures. This world has certain properties, by virtue of its contingency, that make natural evils inevitable. These properties both enable and limit the God who has created the world.

Why did he not create the world with different qualities than it has? Specifically, should he not have created the world so that natural evil would have been ruled out? God cannot be faulted for creating the world as a contingent entity, for he could not have created it otherwise. It is logically impossible for God to create a cosmos of noncontingent things, since for something to be created is, by definition, for that thing to be contingent. Only God's being is noncontingent in its essence. Since it is contingency that introduces change, decay, destruction, and other natural evils, there is no moral blame attributable to God by virtue of their existence.

With regard to a world—within any system of theology or philosophy—there appear to be three possibilities: (1) our present world with its present natural laws; (2) our present world in which deity intervenes constantly to prevent natural evils; or (3) a different world, governed by a set of natural laws different from those presently known to us.

Possibility (2) is not a reasonable alternative. In such a world, it is presumed that the deity involved would ordinarily let events run their natural course. At any point when an unhappy, painful, or otherwise evil result was about to issue from those regularities, however, he would be expected to intervene either to eliminate the untoward thing about to occur or to bring a desirable consequence from the series of preceding events.[6] It seems clear that this would not be a desirable environment. Let me explain:

Rationality is predicated on a high degree of dependability between observable causes and their effects. Even if, as Hume suggested, cause and effect should be held to be nothing more than a psychological phenomenon, we rely on the general apparent regularity of our world to predict possibilities, make rational choices, and evaluate past performance. Given A and B, C is the result; from this we extrapolate to "scientific laws," which enable us to understand, manage, and use our environment constructively.

In a world with constant miraculous intervention, no such rational prediction and use of the environment could occur with the degree of statistical probability we have come to expect and rely on.

> Thus, in a world which operates according to divine miraculous intervention, there would be no necessary relation between phenomena, and in particular between cause and effect. In some instances one event would follow from a certain set of conditions, another time a different event, and so on, such that ultimately an uncountable variety of events would follow a given set of conditions. There would be no regularity of consequence, no natural production of effects. . . . Hence we could not know or even suppose what course of action to take to accomplish a certain rationally conceived goal. Thus, we could neither propose action nor act ourselves.[7]

This sort of environment would hardly be the best of possible worlds. It would not even be a good and desirable world. It would not be the kind of world a benevolent deity would create, for it would only confuse and frustrate its inhabitants who were endowed with rationality.

Since the initial creation of this contingent universe, God's designs and purposes for his creatures have been fulfilled within the arena of history. While the Judeo-Christian system allows for occasional divine interventions for the sake of revelatory encouragements and/or instruction about spiritual and moral duties, it does not have room for a world where divine intervention is the norm.

As to possibility (3), it seems more unreasonable than the one just examined. A different world in which different laws of nature operate can be posited but has yet to be described. As Plantinga points out, "a possible world is any possible state of affairs that is complete."[8] This means that it is too simplistic to say, "A better world would be one in which there is no pain, bees cross-pollinate but do not sting, falling would not result in broken bones, etc." This is too simplistic, for the simple reason that it does not take into account that these things can be accomplished only by changing the world and objects within it so radically that they become something other than what they are. Among other things, man would have to be changed so radically that we would no longer have a *prima facie* right to call him "man."

In order to eliminate pain, for example, the entire nervous system would have to do something other than what we know. Our physical bodies, well adapted as they are to their environment, have nervous systems that allow the experience of pleasure. A concomitant condition of such a sensory mechanism is that it also allows the experience of pain. Can the possibility of pain be eliminated without altering us so radically as to make us something other than human beings (rational animals)?

In other words, the assignment of different specific qualities within our world necessitates more far-reaching alterations than we generally posit. Such a "solution" to the problem of evil therefore creates even greater problems than it sets out to resolve.

There seems to be a significant presumption on the part of the objector to theism who is pressing the problem of evil. Why does he presume that all things that are singly possible (the elimination of pain in human beings) are also compossible—that is, possible in conjunction with the remainder of reality without irreparable harm?

A rational impasse occurs here. The nontheist calls for a world better than this one but cannot describe all the details necessary for its instantiation; it would take omniscience to provide such a description. The theist holds that an omniscient deity knew what the best of all possible worlds (or, at least, as good as any possible world) would be and created it for us. It is neither possible nor logically necessary for a theist to explain how his deity arrived at such a conclusion about possible worlds or to show how every particular evil in this world is justified.

4. A theodicy constructed within the framework of teleology and ethical responsibility must preserve human freedom and its corollary of moral praiseworthiness/blameworthiness.

The entire cosmos must be characterized by certain nonmiraculous features that will allow natural law and the possibility of natural evils if man is to "employ his reason in the conduct of his life. And, without rationality, morality is impossible."[9] Since a universe that contains the *possibility* of evil can be the useful instrument of a divine moral purpose, such a universe is still justified in its existence even if that unpleasant possibility is realized.

God did not create humanity with either a proneness to sin or the predetermined choice of sin. He created us with moral freedom. If this freedom is genuine rather than apparent, then the misuse of that freedom is hardly an indictment of God. Omnipotence is not to be confused with omnicausality. When I abuse my freedom to sin against God or man, *I* am responsible, and *I* am culpable. Since my sinful act was neither predetermined nor otherwise caused by God, the responsibility and culpability cannot be assigned to him.

A Response to the Problem of Evil

The theodicy set forth here begins with a deity who is supreme among all beings in both goodness and power. This God creates a contingent cosmos *ex nihilo* and fashions humanity "in his own image" to be the highest-level animal creature in the cosmos. Humanity is responsible for demonstrating likeness to the Creator by living in the

world by reason (*knowing* the will of God) and with moral
responsibility (*doing* the will of God).

In order for mankind to exercise its rational and ethical
sensibilities, human beings had to be placed in an environment suited to that purpose. Following Hick, we shall say
that this environment needed to be constructed as a suitable place for "soul-making." This term refers to Planet
Earth as a place of challenge to the intellectual, moral, and
spiritual sensibilities of human creatures.

Against the possible rejoinder that God had no right to
place creatures in such an environment of jeopardy (Some
of his creatures may fail the test!), one might think in terms
of a couple of analogies.

Parents sometimes give their children challenging tasks
to perform—some of which may involve a degree of personal danger. Teachers typically give stiff exams and
demanding projects to their students. Yet we do not regard
such parents or teachers as wicked. We see them as challenging the growth potential of their children or students
and attempting to bring out their best possibilities. They
are subjecting them to the sort of discipline and develop-
mental tasks that will make them intellectually and morally stronger.

Exertion, challenge, and the facing of difficulties could
hardly be removed from the world that man inhabits without defeating the divine purpose to bring out the full
potential in human beings. In a world where suffering and
untoward events were eliminated, rational and moral qualities would be only excess baggage without real significance to human nature, responsibility, or behavior.

Trying to imagine some of the features of a world utterly
incapable of experiencing suffering, Hick writes:

> It would mean that no wrong action could ever have bad
> effects, and that no piece of carelessness or ill-judgment in
> dealing with the world could ever lead to harmful conse-
> quences. If a thief were to steal a million pounds from a
> bank, instead of anyone being made poorer thereby, anoth-

er million pounds would appear from nowhere to replenish the safe; and this, moreover, without causing any inflationary consequences. . . . Anyone driving at breakneck speed along a narrow road and hitting a pedestrian would leave his victim miraculously unharmed; or if one slipped and fell through a fifth-floor window, gravity would be partially suspended, and he would float gently to the ground.[10]

While such possibilities could, in fact, be realized in a world created by a God of unlimited power, they could *not* be realized consistent with his intention to have this world serve a soul-making, character-development, purpose. Rationality and morality would cease to have meaning in such a world.

There would be nothing wrong with stealing, because no one would ever lose anything by it; there would be no such crime as murder, because no one could ever be killed. . . . Not only would there be no way in which anyone could injure anyone else, but there would also be no way in which anyone could benefit anyone else, since there would be no possibility of lack or danger.[11]

We sometimes overlook the fact that pain is not always evil. Most often, in fact, it is a good thing in human experience. It is an essential mechanism for our survival. (Among nonrational animals, it may even be the primary mechanism for their survival.) Without the ability to experience pain, our bodies are robbed of protection. How does one know how hot to run the bath water so as not to scald and peel off one's flesh? How does a child playing on the beach know to keep tiny and abrasive sand particles out of his eye so his vision will not be impaired or lost? How does someone with an inflamed appendix know to seek medical help before it is too late? Pain is generally an *instrumental good* in our experience. A theist could even insist that it is part of the wise design of our human bodies by an infinitely good God.

Neither should we regard death as an *intrinsically evil* intruder into our cosmos. To the contrary, the death of physical organisms is necessary to our world. The death of bacteria is required to have fertile soil; the death of plants is required for certain animals to eat and survive; many higher animals depend on the death of lower animals for their survival.

And death must have been inherent in man himself. This is true not only for the evolutionist, who sees mankind's development through struggle, death, and the survival of the fittest, but also for the biblical theist. What reason does anyone have for thinking Adam would not have died physically, even if he had not sinned and he had remained in Eden? Could he not have drowned while swimming or been crushed under a tree he was cutting down? Access to the "tree of life" would have apparently spared him from death as the result of aging and physical deterioration (cf. Gen. 3:22–23), but there is no good reason to assume it would have made him into a "superman" who could not be harmed—even killed—by accident or natural disaster. It would not have been desirable, given the earth's limited resources, for there to have been no physical death among human beings from Adam's time to our own.

The death that came as a direct result of the sin of Adam and Eve was the *spiritual* death (the separation from divine fellowship) they experienced "in the day" they ate of the forbidden tree (cf. Gen 2:17). Adam's physical death was, at most, an indirect consequence of his sin.

Pain is *not* an evidence against God's existence, power, or love. Death is *not* intrinsically evil. Both pain and death can serve good as well as bad purposes in human experiences. Sin—moral evil that results from the abuse of freedom—is the only intrinsic evil in human experience.

God superintends the cosmos, but he does not coerce it by refusing to allow situations where natural evil can occur. Given the existence of an ordered cosmos and the divine purpose of providing an ideal environment for soul-making, the events we term natural evils are concomitant conditions of its existence. *God is, therefore, not morally blameworthy for allowing the world to come into being so as to contain natural evil, for he did so consistent with a morally praiseworthy goal.*

Having created a world with a teleological motive, God must deal with its material essence in terms of its inherent properties. Two of those features involve law-like regularities governing contingent substances. These features are sufficient of themselves to account for most of the natural evils we face in the cosmos. Materiality and its inherent features are neither sinister nor evil in themselves. Thus, it follows that God is not compromised with regard to power, for changing the nature of matter and its qualities would mean creating a world essentially different from this one. Neither is he compromised with regard to goodness for the very meaning of moral action can be derived only from a world such as this one.

Coupled with the nature of contingent reality, there is the matter of circumstantial freedom required in order for the world to be a soul-making environment which occasions many natural evils. There must be, for example, freedom enough for men to make mistakes.[12]

A group of well-trained engineers may design a passenger jet with great care and professional diligence. Yet they may calculate incorrectly the amount of stress a crucial section of the wing will be forced to bear under certain conditions and, thus, create an instrument of death. A physician may administer a specific antibiotic to cure a woman's throat infection and have to watch her die from an unforeseeably severe allergic reaction to the drug given her. Any number of decisions we make about school, investments, or personal relationships can result in immense suffering for ourselves and/or others due to our inability to know the innumerable contingencies related to them.

Due to the natural requirements of heating and cooling, the earth's crust shifts to reveal and make available to us great mineral deposits, which enable our quality of life to improve. Yet the same system of plate movements occasionally causes devastating earthquakes in populated areas. An event that is neither good nor bad in itself can therefore be an instrumental source of both good and bad. The same observation can be made about natural and life-giving processes in the atmosphere, which cleanse the air of harmful impurities but may also cause flooding. Complicating these natural processes with their occasional unfortunate outcomes is man's unintentional harm to his environment by such things as overpopulating an area and creating food shortages, over-grazing or poor cultivation techniques that turn good soil into desert, and the like.

The ultimate complication in this scenario is man's intentional harm to others through the misuse of his moral freedom. Thus, some people steal, murder, and lie. God is not an omnicausal agent who has driven them to their actions. He is a benevolent Creator who has given a good gift (moral freedom) to his creatures, only to suffer himself at its perversion.

God's Entry into Human Suffering

How could a divine being experience and understand suffering? How could he share in the limitations of contingency and be a victim of humanity's misuse of moral freedom? Christian theology answers these questions by pointing to the experience of Jesus of Nazareth.

In Jesus Christ we see the ultimate divine response to the human predicament. The God who created all things, and for whose glory they exist, subjected himself to natural laws and human vulnerability. He took the pain of his creation to himself. He became hungry and tired, wept over the death of a friend, knew the agony of being lied about and betrayed, and experienced death. Because of the experiences Jesus had, Christians affirm that our suffering elicits his compassion. "For we do not have a high priest who is unable to sympathize with our weaknesses, but we have one who has been tempted in every way, just as we are—yet was without sin" (Heb. 4:15).

The God whom Christians believe in is "the Father of compassion and the God of all comfort" (2 Cor. 1:3). So, when bad things happen and we are tempted to lash out at God, accuse him, or think he has forgotten us, Christian faith allows trusting people to adopt a positive attitude: "Consider it pure joy, my brothers, whenever you face trials of many kinds, because you know that the testing of your faith develops perseverance [steadfastness, RSV]" (James 1:2–3).

Conclusion

There are no victories without battles. Character develops only as it is tested by the experiences of living. These testing experiences show us our need for God and can drive us closer to him rather than away from him.

God's grace in a believer's life is not intended to save him from trouble. It is intended to save him from defeat. Understanding that life is best measured in nearness to God, instead of in the externals of this life, changes the way one looks at life in general. Anything that takes one away from God is evil—even if pleasurable, exciting, and done in the context of comfort. Everything that brings one nearer to God—even if unpleasant at the time—is good. From this perspective, then, suffering does not disallow the possibility of faith, but makes it only more reasonable.

5

Looking *at* the Bible

Only the question of the existence of God is more fundamental than the issue of the origin, nature, and authority of
the Bible.

Chapters 2 through 4 of this book have argued a rational
case for the existence of a personal Supreme Being. At the
point when one comes to believe in the existence of God, it
is immediately reasonable—if not necessary—that one ask:
Would such a being not reveal himself to his creatures?
Might he not seek to communicate with man?

Vladimir A. Soloukhin is a Russian essayist and poet
who has been a member of the Communist Party for well
over thirty years. He wrote a few years back in the Soviet
journal *Kommunist* that "in the twentieth century, there is
no doubt for every reasonable person that a supreme reason exists in the world, in the universe, in life." His article
closes with the affirmation that a denial of higher reason
behind the cosmos would be to say that such "complicated
and precise organisms as a flower, a bird, a human being
and, finally, a human brain, appeared at random—the
result of a lucky, blind and unprogrammed combination of
chemical elements. . . . The question is not *whether a
supreme reason exists, but whether it knows about me and has
anything to do with me.*"[1]

Soloukhin has raised the ultimate issue of theism: the

possibility of a relationship with our Creator. If such a relationship is possible, it will have to involve communication between deity and humanity. Indeed, the Christian religion claims that God has reached out to man through both the *written Word* and the *incarnate Word*: "In the past God spoke to our forefathers through the prophets at many times and in various ways, but in these last days he has spoken to us by his Son, whom he appointed heir of all things, and through whom he made the universe" (Heb. 1:1).

The remainder of this book focuses on these two alleged revelations of God. Since the Old and New Testament documents are part of the data required to make the case for the deity of Jesus Christ, we will look first at the argument for Scripture as the Word of God and then move to the case for the deity of Christ.

Humankind needs a revelation from God in understandable human language. Nature reveals God's wisdom, power, and personality, but it does not reveal his will for the men and women created in his image. Nature does not answer the questions in our minds about our relationship with God. If he had remained silent, concealed in the thick darkness of human ignorance and superstition, our plight would be desperate. The Christian religion affirms that God has indeed spoken to us through Scripture and has dispersed darkness with divine light.

If God has revealed himself in propositional form (in words and statements), that revelation could reasonably be expected to reflect certain properties. For one thing, the infinite knowledge and moral perfection of the deity would mean that any revelation from him would *be entirely true* in all its particulars; his omniscience would prevent errors from lack of knowledge, and his truthfulness would keep him from lies and deception. Also, one would expect any revelation from God to *be coherent* and thus a unity in all its various parts—not self-contradictory. It could reasonably be expected to *contain his will* for his creatures so as to instruct them in how to be fit for his fellowship.

Finally, it would also be expected to *provide motivation* for faith in and obedience to its contents.

In the next four chapters, it will be argued that the Bible and the Bible alone exhibits the qualities appropriate to a revelation from God. Any book that claims to be a revelation from God ought to be examined on its own merits. Intellectual honesty demands as much. Does the Bible claim to be God-given and inerrant? What traits does Scripture have that bear on such a claim? Do these traits confirm or deny the claim? What objections do unbelievers lodge against the Bible as a divine revelation? These are the issues we will examine in chapters 5 through 8.

The Claims of the Bible

It would be presumptuous to claim that the Bible is a divine revelation if the book nowhere alleges as much for itself. On the other hand, making a claim to divine origin would not be enough of itself to prove the claim to be true. So the first order of business is to get clear about the Bible's claims for itself.

The Old Testament Views Itself

The preeminent personality of the Old Testament is Moses. In the Book of Exodus, an interesting account is given of his call to be the deliverer of the Israelites from their captivity in Egypt. Having been an exile from Egypt for about forty years, Moses was living in Midian. He had married, started his family, and settled into the life of a nomadic herdsman.

Moses' desert life was interrupted by a divine call. Then, when he claimed a lack of experience in public affairs and lamented that he would not know what to say before Pharaoh, he was given this assurance: "The LORD said to him, 'Who gave man his mouth? Who makes him deaf or mute? Who gives him sight or makes him blind? Is it not I, the LORD? Now go; *I will help you speak and will teach you what to say*'" (Exod. 4:11–12, italics added). Moses would not have questioned the power of Yahweh (the covenant name of the God of Israel) to create, give or take the powers of speech and sight, and so forth. Thus, he was asked to believe that God's divine power could control and guide the content of his speech before Pharaoh.

The Old Testament also claims that Moses wrote under the same supernatural direction that accompanied his spoken messages. "Then the LORD said to Moses, 'Write down these words, for in accordance with these words I have made a covenant with you and with Israel' " (Exod. 34:27; cf. 17:14; 24:4; Num. 33:2; Deut. 31:9).

In the Pentateuch (the first five books of the Old Testament, all of which are attributed to Mosaic authorship), it is stated no fewer than 420 times that the express words of God are being recounted.

Moses is not the only Old Testament personality for whom the claim is made that he is speaking or writing for God. For example, the formula "Thus says the Lord" or its equivalent appears nearly eighty times in the Book of Isaiah. And Jeremiah recounted his call to a prophetic ministry this way: "Then the LORD reached out his hand and *touched my mouth* and said to me, 'Now, *I have put my words in your mouth*'" (Jer. 1:9, italics added).

The consistent claim of all the Hebrew prophets is that they spoke only when God revealed his word to them (cf. Hos. 1:1; Amos 1:3; Mic. 1:1; Mal. 1:1; *et al.*).

One of the most interesting of the prophetic calls is that of Amos. Following the division of the nation into two kingdoms after Solomon's death, he was a native of the Southern Kingdom (Judah) whose principal task was to prophesy to the Northern Kingdom (Israel). During the period around 760–750 B.C., Amos was emphatic in calling the people of Israel to a sense of social justice. Yet he had no background in either the prophetic or priestly line. When challenged about his credentials, he said, "I was neither a prophet nor a prophet's son, but I was a shepherd, and I also took care of sycamore-fig trees. But the LORD took me from tending the flock and said to me, 'Go, prophesy to my people Israel.' Now then, hear the word of the LORD . . ." (Amos 7:14–16a).

The New Testament Views the Old

Jesus, his apostles, and the prophets of the early church affirmed their conviction that the Old Testament documents were from God.

Jesus' attitude toward the divine origin of Scripture is clear from his statements about and appeals to it.

> Do not think that I have come to abolish the Law or the Prophets; I have not come to abolish them but to fulfill them. I tell you the truth, until heaven and earth disappear, not the smallest letter, not the least stroke of a pen, will by any means disappear from the Law until everything is accomplished (Matt. 5:17–18).
>
> But about the resurrection from the dead—have you not read what God said to you, "I am the God of Abraham, the God of Isaac, and the God of Jacob"? (Matt. 22:31–32).
>
> . . . the Scripture cannot be broken (John 10:35b).

Jesus read the Old Testament. He quoted it. He lived by its commandments. He challenged others to study and believe it. It is significant that he never once quoted from any noncanonical book or assigned divine authority to any writings other than those of the Old Testament. He never called a single passage of the Old Testament into question or felt compelled to correct anything in it.

Some of the most disputed parts of the Old Testament narrative are judged historic by Jesus, based on their inclusion in the Old Testament. He believed in the real existence of an original couple from whom all humans have descended (Matt. 19:4), affirmed the reality of the flood of Noah's day (Matt. 24:37–39), regarded as historical the biblical story about the destruction of Sodom by fire from heaven (Luke 17:28–32), attested the miraculous healing of people who fixed their gaze on the brass serpent set up by

Moses in the desert (John 3:14), and spoke of the record of
Jonah's three days and nights in the belly of a great fish as
historical (Matt. 12:39–40). There is no doubt that Jesus
regarded the Old Testament as God-given and authoritative. He expressed total trust in Scripture.

Paul, the great first-century evangelist and theologian,
expressed what seems to be the typical attitude of the early
church toward the Old Testament. *"All Scripture is God-
breathed* and is useful for teaching, rebuking, correcting
and training in righteousness, so that the man of God may
be thoroughly equipped for every good work"* (2 Tim.
3:16–17, italics added). In articulating the relationship of
God to the written words of Scripture, he used the Greek
term *theopneustos.* Translated "inspired by God" in the RSV
and "God-breathed" in the NIV, the word makes a clear and
explicit claim for the Old Testament.

Peter affirmed the same doctrine of divine origin for
Scripture. "Above all, you must understand that *no prophecy of Scripture came about by the prophet's own interpretation,"*
he wrote—"For prophecy never had its origin in the will of
man, but *men spoke from God as they were carried along by the
Holy Spirit"* (2 Peter 1:20–21, italics added). The Greek
word translated "carried along" in this text (*phero*) is the
same one used at Acts 27:17 to describe a ship that was
"driven" or "carried along" by the strong winds of a
storm. In other words, Peter believed that the human writers of Scripture no more determined the ultimate course of
their writings than a ship could choose its own course
when being carried by strong winds on the ocean.

This fact raises an important point about the doctrine of
"inspiration." Inspiration is a process, and the word
inspired properly refers not to the writer but to the finished
product. Thus, Christian scholars over the centuries have
used the term *verbal inspiration* of this process. For the sake
of clarity, however, a note of caution needs to be sounded
about this term.

Verbal inspiration does not necessarily mean mechanical
dictation, as if the writers of Scripture were only passive

participants in the process. The term refers to the extent of the process and affirms that inspiration extended to the very words on the completed page and not merely to the general substance of those words.

Viewed as a process, inspiration involved a combination of divine power and human instrumentality. As presented within the Bible itself, the process allowed God to make use of the natural gifts of the individual writers (their background, temperament, vocabulary, style) and, at the same time, direct them by the power of the Holy Spirit in order to enable them to communicate his will without admixture of error. The divine element was primary and the human secondary, but they were joined to produce a totally trustworthy revelation of divine truth through human authors.

The process occasionally involved a degree of dictation. In certain Old Testament settings, for example, God is represented as speaking and simply having a man to record his words—allowing the writer to be his recording secretary (Gen. 22:15–18; Exod. 20:1–17). In the New Testament, the letters to the seven churches of Asia are represented as having been dictated to John by the resurrected Christ (Rev. 2:1, 8, 12, 18; 3:1, 7, 14).

There are other times when inspiration involved a direct communication from the Lord without any explanation of the method involved (1 Cor. 11:23).

Writers sometimes received revelation in the form of a vision whose meaning was then made plain to them by the involvement of the Holy Spirit (Acts 10:9–16)

There are some circumstances where the inspiration process guaranteed only an accurate record of events or statements without any endorsement of what was recorded. For example, the sins of God's people (1 Cor. 1:11) and the evil deeds of people against the earliest Christians (Acts 6:11–14) are recorded with historical accuracy but certainly without approval or justification.

On still other occasions, writers had to use their own energies and skills in doing careful research (Luke 1:1–4) or were allowed to express their deepest personal feelings about a given situation (Rom. 10:1; cf. Ps. 51). Even in these instances, however, the process of inspiration claims that the Holy Spirit so controlled the entire process that the writing was kept free of error. At the end of the process, what had been produced could be called *God's* Word on the matter.

It was out of their conviction that they were being guided directly by God in their work that the framers of Scripture could claim divine authority for their statements. Again, however, *merely making the claim to direct divine guidance in their work does not guarantee the truthfulness of that claim. Its proof or disproof must come from our subsequent inductive study of the phenomena of the Bible.* At this point, we are simply trying to document and understand the nature of the claim.

The New Testament Views Itself

Having looked at the Old Testament's claims for itself and the New Testament's claims for the Old Testament, the final thing to be done in this section is to show some of the claims that the New Testament makes for itself.

The New Testament's claim to inspiration and authority is founded in promises that Jesus made to his disciples. Anticipating that they would generate opposition in their work, he said, "But when they arrest you, do not worry about what to say or how to say it. At that time *you will be given what to say, for it will not be you speaking, but the Spirit of your Father speaking through you*" (Matt. 10:19–20, italics added; cf. Luke 21:12–15).

Beyond the promise of verbal guidance before their enemies, Jesus made this pact with them about their work as his ambassadors: "But the Counselor, the Holy Spirit, whom the Father will send in my name, will *teach you all things* and will *remind you of everything I have said to you*" (John 14:26, italics added; cf. 16:13).

In summary of these promises, Jesus pledged that his selected representatives (1) would be provided with the

very words with which to defend themselves before their
critics and enemies; (2) would be enabled to recall accurately the things Jesus had said while still among them in
person; and (3) would be given additional revelation
beyond what Jesus had personally communicated. All
these promises were contingent on an empowering by the
Holy Spirit, which he promised them.

On the Pentecost Day following Jesus' crucifixion in A.D.
30, Peter claimed that the Holy Spirit had been "poured
out" in fulfillment of promise. The remainder of the Book
of Acts documents the teaching and confirmatory signs the
apostles and evangelists of the first church offered the
world.

Paul disclaimed either "eloquence or superior wisdom"
in his teaching and attributed its origin to the power of the
Holy Spirit (1 Cor. 2:1–4). In an interesting discussion of
what he claimed to be the source of his message, he wrote:

However, as it is written:
   "No eye has seen,
      no ear has heard,
   no mind has conceived
      what God has prepared for those who love him"—
but God has revealed it to us by his Spirit.

The Spirit searches all things, even the deep things of God.
For who among men knows the thoughts of a man except
the man's spirit within him? In the same way no one knows
the thoughts of God except the Spirit of God. We have not
received the spirit of the world but the Spirit who is from
God, that we may understand what God has freely given
us. This is what we speak, not in words taught us by
human wisdom but *in words taught by the Spirit*, expressing
spiritual truths in spiritual words (1 Cor. 2:9–13, italics
added).

It was his confidence in the process of divine inspiration
that allowed Paul to affirm that his message was to be
accepted "not as the word of men, but as it actually is, *the*

word of God" (1 Thess. 2:13, italics added). And he unequiv-
ocally claimed the authority of Christ for his written words
when he said: "If anybody thinks he is a prophet or spiritually gifted, let him acknowledge that *what I am writing to
you is the Lord's command*" (1 Cor. 14:37, italics added).

Peter claimed nothing less than Paul for himself and his
fellow apostles. Writing to Christians who were being tested in their loyalty to the faith they had embraced, he
reminded them that the apostles "have *preached the gospel
to you by the Holy Spirit* sent from heaven" (1 Peter 1:12b,
italics added). In a second letter to the same group of people, Peter encouraged them to give attention to certain
exhortations that "our dear brother *Paul also wrote you with
the wisdom that God gave him*" (2 Peter 3:15b). He proceeded
to refer to "all his [Paul's] letters" as being on par with
"the other *Scriptures*" known to his readers from the Old
Testament documents (v. 16).

The view of the Bible to be defended in this book
involves the high claim of *verbal inspiration* and *infallibility*.
Human beings think and communicate in words. Thus, if
there has been or is to be any genuine communication of
his will from the mind of God to the minds of men, that
communication has to involve the very words used in it.

Only recently have some people argued that the Bible
can be from God, yet errant. From God's own nature as
truth, however, follows the corollary that if the Bible *is* the
Word of God—rather than a mere witness to him or a book
that contains God's words—then it must be truthful and
authoritative in all its parts. If the Bible is the Word of God
in whole and in its parts, it must be entirely truthful,
because God himself is truthful.

Some students of the Bible argue for a type of inspiration by means of which God gave truth to men in the
forms of *infallible ideas* but left them to express those ideas
in their own *fallible words*. But this puts us back at square
one with regard to knowing the mind of God. If God did
not control the choice of the words being used by the
apostles, prophets, and evangelists who produced

Scripture, we have no basis for secure confidence that "revelation" (making known something that had not been known previously, unveiling something that had been hidden) has taken place at all.

Apart from divine guidance from beginning to end in the process, we would have no way of knowing how adequately (or inadequately) the people involved expressed the thoughts they were given. As Benjamin Warfield expressed it: "Revelation is but half revelation unless it be infallibly communicated; it is but half communicated unless it be infallibly recorded."[2]

Two Types of Evidence

It would be a peculiar form of circular reasoning to affirm that the Bible is inspired of God and true because it claims to be so and that the truthfulness of such a claim can be granted because the claim is made in an inspired and true book. Having established the claim, however, it remains for us to examine the relevant evidence.

There are two types of information that bear on the issue we are examining: *external evidences of inspiration* and *internal evidences of inspiration*.

External evidence that the Bible is a divine production comes from sources such as history, geography, archaeology, and the natural sciences. Taken collectively, the many bits of data from these sources that confirm the factual accuracy of both Old and New Testaments go far in removing a person's reluctance to believe that the Bible is from God.

At the same time, however, one must realize that a book could be factually accurate without being produced by God. It is theoretically possible that a directory of 10,000 names, addresses, and phone numbers is factually correct with every entry. That would not prove that the people who produced it were guided by God.

A technical way to state the significance of external evidences of the Bible's inspiration is to say that they are nec-

essary to the case but insufficient of themselves to establish
it. In the final analysis, the only sufficient evidence of
divine inspiration is to be found in some form of arresting
internal evidence. There must be one or more features of
the Bible that are so unique that they are incapable of
explanation apart from God's involvement in the process.
Some of these phenomena will be studied in chapter 6.

External Evidences of Divine Origin

The past few decades have witnessed a remarkable
resurgence of interest in the Bible. Following a time when
it was fashionable to criticize the Bible for its anachronisms, historical blunders, and errors of fact, there has
been a radical change in attitudes toward Scripture. A host
of things that have come to light in scholarly research has
finally filtered into the popular press. More and more people are being prodded by these facts to reexamine the Bible
as a divine revelation.

Several years ago, *Time* magazine featured the following
question on its front cover: "How True Is the Bible?" The
magazine's cover story article offered its answer to the
question by saying that "the Bible is often surprisingly
accurate in historical particulars, more so than earlier generations of scholars ever suspected."[3] On the final page of
an eight-page article, the piece concluded:

After more than two centuries of facing the heaviest scientific guns that could be brought to bear, the Bible has survived—and is perhaps the better for the siege.

Even on the critics' own terms—historical fact—the
Scriptures seem more acceptable now than they did when
the rationalists began the attack. Noting one example
among many, New Testament Scholar Bruce Metzger
observes that the *Book of Acts* was once accused of historical
errors for details that have since been proved by archaeologists and historians to be correct.[4]

Staying with the popular press, a similar article was published early in the 1980s in still another national newsmagazine. "A wave of archaeological discoveries is altering old ideas about the roots of Christianity and Judaism—and affirming that the Bible is more historically accurate than many scholars thought."[5]

That the quotations above are from widely known newsmagazines rather than technical journals shows the impact that modern scientific research—especially archaeology—has had in confirming the Bible's reliability on matters of historical fact. Such magazines have no theological axe to grind and simply report on a popular level what is generally known among students of both Scripture and history.

The Bible has not undergone change in the last hundred years. But advances in scholarship have caused attitudes toward it to change dramatically during that century. The excessive skepticism that was in vogue has been in constant retreat before the discoveries of archaeology.

The Bible is written within the arena of history, and its great doctrines are grounded in the historical facts to which it bears witness. If the Bible errs in matters of history, how can we have confidence in its general reliability as a revelation from God? If research confirms the credibility of its writers, however, their integrity is enhanced when they claim to speak with divine authority on an issue.

External Evidences: Old Testament

Archaeology has discovered people, events, and whole civilizations that were previously known to us only from the Bible. Based on the silence of records other than Scripture, critics were quick to allege that the Bible was in error. Yet, with the passing of time and by the unearthing of more data, the Bible has been vindicated repeatedly. Nelson Glueck, a respected Jewish archaeologist, has claimed: "It may be stated categorically that no archaeological discovery has ever controverted a biblical reference."[6]

For instance, critics of the Bible once pointed to the several Old Testament references to the Hittites and expressed the opinion that they were the mythical creation of late Hebrew writers. In 1906, a German archaeologist named Winckler unearthed the capital city of the Hittite empire and found huge archives of cuneiform (wedge-shaped writing) tablets. The entire body of Hittite history learned from those tablets confirms the biblical record of their place in Hebrew history.

Critics had also said that the cultural conditions in Palestine were unlike those described in the Bible at the time Abraham was supposed to have lived. They denied the historicity of Sargon of Assyria. The historical context of the life of Abraham now stands confirmed, and the palace of Sargon has been discovered and excavated at Khorsabad. Time and time again, this sort of thing has happened—always to the Bible's vindication.

Detractors had once challenged the biblical representation of Solomon's wealth and splendor. In particular, they had assumed flagrant exaggerations in the Book of 1 Kings in its descriptions of him. There he is said to have been a great builder who had access to equipment for refining metal (chs. 7–8), to have had a navy (9:26), to have had a vast number of horses and chariots (10:26), and so forth. How could the king of little, insignificant Palestine have attained the wealth and power assigned him in the Bible? Unbelievers dismissed the claims as a combination of embellishments and myths.

Archaeological digs into the ruins of cities contemporary with Solomon's reign (970–930 B.C.) have provided evidence to substantiate every biblical claim. For example, recent work by Pritchard at Tell es-Saidiyeh, east of the Jordan River, has disclosed several open smelting pits. Suitable ores for use in those pits have been found in the adjacent Arabah Valley. Nelson Glueck had previously revealed the location of several copper mines in the same valley location. Beno Rothenberg found still more smelting sites and showed how the copper-bearing ores of the region were smelted in open pits on charcoal fires fanned by bellows.

That Solomon indeed had a navy—with Phoenician help from Hiram of Tyre—and sent expeditions to bring back gold from Ophir (cf. 2 Chron. 8:17–18) is validated by an eighth-century ostracon found just north of Tel Avid—"gold from Ophir for Beth Horon, 30 shekels."

Structures built to accommodate Solomon's cavalry have been found at Hazor, Taanach, and Jerusalem. A mistranslation of 1 Kings 10:28 in the King James Version obscures the fact that Solomon was securing his horses from a region in southeast Turkey where the best horses of the time were to be found. A word translated "linen yarn" in the KJV should read "from Cilicia"; thus the verse says: "And Solomon's horses were imported from Egypt and Cilicia" ("Kue," NIV).

Solomon was not an insignificant king over an insignificant people. In fact, he reigned with all the splendor, wealth, and far-reaching influence assigned him in the biblical texts. Substantiating evidence outside the Bible verifies his grandeur as a ruler.

The Book of Daniel has also been a major focus of criticism by unbelievers. In particular, his description of King Belshazzar's feast (Dan. 5:1ff) was considered totally unhistorical. Porphyry, a third-century enemy of the Christian religion who produced the infamous *Against the Christians*, advanced the theory that Daniel was written about 165 B.C. (long after the facts it alleges to describe in the sixth century B.C.), was worthless as history, and was filled with kings (Belshazzar) who were fictional. This view of Daniel became the standard judgment of the book during the nineteenth century's rise of critical scholarship. But:

Then, in 1854, a British consul named J. G. Taylor explored some ruins in southern Iraq on behalf of the British Museum. He dug into a great mud-brick tower that was part of a temple of the moon god that dominated the city.

Taylor found several small clay cylinders buried in the brickwork, each about four inches long, inscribed with 60 or so lines of cuneiform writing. . . .

The inscriptions had been written at the command of Nabonidus, king of Babylon from 555 to 539 B.C. The king had repaired the temple tower, and the clay cylinders commemorated that fact. The inscriptions proved that the ruined tower was the temple of the city of Ur. The words were a prayer for the long life and good health of Nabonidus—and for his eldest son. The name of that son, clearly written, was Belshazzar![7]

Here was clear proof that Belshazzar had lived in Babylon at the time Daniel alleged. In fact, since 1854 several more Babylonian documents that mention Belshazzar have been discovered.

While the Bible's critics were somewhat chagrined over these finds, they remained content to point out that the references speak of him as King Nabonidus's son or the crown prince. The title "king" is not ascribed to him. Thus, Daniel was alleged to be factually incorrect on the status of Belshazzar. However:

A very recent discovery may throw additional light on Belshazzar's status. In 1979, a farmer in northern Syria, while plowing, accidentally uncovered a life-size statue of a king of ancient Gozan. On the skirt of the statue are two inscriptions, one in Assyrian and the other in Aramaic, both written at the same time, probably about 850 B.C. The inscriptions, in two different languages, are parallel, nearly identical, and each helps to interpret the other. The Assyrian text describes the ruler on whose statue the inscription is written as the "governor of Gozan"; the Aramaic text describes him as "king" (mlk). Each inscription was aimed at a different audience, the Assyrian version to the overlords, and the Aramaic to the local people. What to the Assyrian-speaking overlords was the governor was to the local Aramaic-speaking population the equivalent of king. The texts on this statue may well indicate that Belshazzar's title in the Aramaic in which Daniel is written was not a literal rendering of his Babylonian title, which was crown prince.

In the light of the Babylonian sources and of the new texts on the statue, it may have been considered quite in order for such unofficial records as the Book of Daniel to call Belshazzar "king." He acted as king, his father's agent, although he may not have been legally king. The precise distinction would have been irrelevant and confusing in the story as related in Daniel.[8]

If this is the correct solution to the status of Belshazzar, it seems to solve a puzzle in the story of Belshazzar's feast. When the mysterious hand wrote on the wall at the feast, Belshazzar offered a reward to the Babylonian wise men or Daniel if one of them could interpret its meaning. The reward included, among other things, being made "the third highest ruler in the kingdom" (Dan. 5:16). If Belshazzar had been king, why would the reward not have been to be *second* ruler in the kingdom? (cf. Gen. 41:40, 44). The answer seems to be that he was not in a position to offer that position without displacing himself. Nabonidus, the father of Belshazzar, was actually king; Belshazzar was the second ruler, or crown prince, who exercised the effective authority in Babylon; Daniel and the Babylonian wise men could be offered only the position of third-highest ruler, behind both Nabonidus and Belshazzar in the empire.

External Evidences: New Testament

Moving from the Old Testament to the New Testament, there is no more arresting case of archaeological confirmation of Scripture than a series of discoveries relating to the two sections written by Luke (the Gospel of Luke and Acts of the Apostles). Around a hundred years ago, with biblical studies dominated largely by the views of F. C. Baur and the Tübingen school of German critical scholars, Acts was generally held to be a second-century document written by a third-rate historian whose dogmatism allowed him little concern for accuracy in historical detail. A radical reversal of attitude toward Acts traces largely to the careful research of the late Sir William Ramsay.

At the beginning of a distinguished career that would make him the foremost authority of his time on the geography and history of Asia Minor in antiquity, Ramsay accepted the general view of Acts, which was derived from the German critics and their Hegelian approach to the development of early Christianity. In *The Bearing of Recent Discovery on the Trustworthiness of the New Testament*, Ramsay describes his eye-opening experience with the Lukan materials:

> Among other old books that described journeys in Asia Minor the Acts of the Apostles had to be read anew. I began to do so without expecting any information of value regarding the condition of Asia Minor at the time when Paul was living. I had read a good deal of modern criticism about the book, and dutifully accepted the current opinion that it was written during the second half of the second century by an author who wished to influence the minds of people in his own time by a highly wrought and imaginative description of the early Church. His object was not to present a trustworthy picture of the facts in the period about A.D. 50, but to produce a certain effect on his own time by setting forth a carefully coloured account of events and persons of that older period. He wrote for his contemporaries, not for truth. He cared nought for geographical or historical surroundings of the period A.D. 30 to 60. He thought only of the period A.D. 160–180, and how he might paint the heroes of old time in situations that should touch the conscience of his contemporaries. Antiquarian or geographical truth was less than valueless in a design like this: one who thought of such things was distracting his attention from the things that really mattered, the things that would move the minds of men in the second century.[9]

The first thing that called into question the assumptions Ramsay had brought to Acts of the Apostles was a discovery pertaining to a geographical statement in Acts 14.

Verse six tells how Paul and Barnabas learned of a plot
against their lives at Iconium "and fled to the Lycaonian
cities of Lystra and Derbe and to the surrounding country."
The language implies that Iconium belonged to a different
country than Lystra and Derbe. Would one speak of leaving Chicago to get to Illinois? Yet historians of Ramsay's
time held, based on information from Cicero and Pliny the
Elder, that Iconium belonged to the region of Lycaonia.
They therefore held that this detail in Acts about border
crossing "was deliberately invented by the writer (who
was under a false impression about the situation of
Iconium and the frontier) with the intention of imparting
to the story plausibility and the interest of personal experience."[10]

However, close inspection of the evidence proved the
accuracy of the biblical text in the matter. Ramsay discovered and proved to the satisfaction of scholars in general
that Iconium belonged to Phrygia during the period A.D.
37–72. Both before and after that time, it was included in
Lycaonia. A topographical border was indeed crossed by
Paul and Barnabas. Only someone from the time of Paul
who cared for accuracy of detail would have gotten the
record straight on such a matter as this.

In this same connection, Ramsay also showed that the
people of Phrygia and Lycaonia were of different racial
stocks and spoke different languages. This confirms the
accuracy of detail exhibited by the writer in logging the
additional detail that the people of Lystra shouted at Paul
"in the Lycaonian language" (Acts 14:11).[11]

The critics had been wrong. It was they who had spoken
out of ignorance rather than the author of Acts of the
Apostles. If the writer of Acts was precisely accurate in
these points, it should not be considered unreasonable to
think him a careful man on other matters. Armed with this
hypothesis, Ramsay pursued his research with vigor.

> Now the condemnation which, as soon as it was tested in
> respect of one detail, had been proved hasty and false, evi-

dently could not be relied on in respect of other details without being tested. Fresh examination of the whole question was needed. The reasons and grounds for our unfavorable judgment regarding the book of Acts must be reconsidered. Prejudice must be set aside. Ignorance of the circumstances of every event must so far as possible be replaced by knowledge through fuller study. Every condition had to be revealed. Every point had to be scrutinized again.[12]

Ramsay's extensive study of the book caused him to change his attitude dramatically toward Acts. He came to advocate a first-century date for the book and also to defend its Lukan authorship. He not only came to trust the historicity of the book himself and to regard it as unsurpassed for its accuracy of detail, his published findings altered the landscape of scholarly attitude toward Acts.

A. N. Sherwin-White, a respected classical historian at Oxford, has reviewed the question of the historical trustworthiness of Acts and affirmed: "For Acts the confirmation of historicity is overwhelming."[13] He added that "any attempt to reject its basic historicity even in matters of detail must now appear absurd."[14]

Conclusion

We cannot elevate our faith in the Bible as the Word of God to the level of what in chapter 1 was called a *substantive belief* or a *justified and true belief* without putting Scripture to the test. Its claims must be delineated carefully and examined critically. But its claims cannot be tested without delving deeply into history and archaeology—disciplines that are neutral to the issue of Christianity and its truth claims.

Perhaps some believers have avoided "secular studies" because of their neutrality. Others may have stayed away from them out of fear that their conclusions from these research areas could undermine their faith. Serious study and careful scholarship can be terribly unsettling to ignorance, prejudice, and shallow dogmatism, but they are not enemies to the Christian faith.

From this chapter, then, we can conclude that the Bible claims divine inspiration for itself and that it exhibits the type of factual accuracy one would expect to find in a book whose ultimate author is a God of intelligence and integrity. It remains, however, to go still another step to find in Scripture some unique feature(s) that can be explained in no way other than divine activity. That will be the burden of proof undertaken in the following chapter.

6

Looking *in* the Bible

No book in the world even begins to approach the Bible in terms of circulation and popularity. According to information from the United Bible Society as of December 31, 1987, complete books of the Bible have been published in 1,884 different languages. The entire Bible has been published in 303 languages, the complete New Testament in 670 languages, and portions of Scripture in 911 other languages and dialects. New translations and study editions of the Bible are appearing constantly. It continues to be the best-selling book in the English language year after year.

More than that, the influence of the Bible has touched every aspect of human experience. Much of the world's great art and music centers on biblical incidents and personalities. The great literature of the world is perfused with quotations from and allusions to Judeo-Christian Scripture.

If the Bible is merely a human document, how can we explain this sort of popularity and influence? In this chapter, we will move from looking at some external evidences of its divine origin to its unique internal features, which prove that Scripture is from God.

The Unity of Scripture

Written in sixty-six sections by about forty different people from a wide variety of backgrounds over a time span of sixteen hundred years on three continents (Europe, Asia, and Africa) and in three languages (Hebrew, Aramaic, and Greek), the Bible is nonetheless a single volume. It tells one unfolding story of the redemption of fallen man with a total harmony of parts. It is not a mere anthology of religious writings, for there is a unity binding it together that no anthology has.

If you just imagine the difficulty you would have in trying to find ten educators, politicians, or scientists to write articles on some controversial subject without contradicting each other, you will begin to appreciate the unanimity of view expressed by the forty different writers of the Bible. If you were to further complicate the process by letting your writers range from fisherman to head of state to prisoner of war, you would abandon the project before starting.

A thousand men may work on a great cathedral, and even take centuries to build it, but if it comes out a work of art, the foundation fittingly suited to the minarets, spires and windows, it is certain there was an architect back of the planning and building.
. . . If a fragment of stone were found in Italy, another in Asia Minor, another in Greece, another in Egypt, and on and on until sixty-six fragments had been found, and if when put together they fitted perfectly together, making a perfect statue of Venus de Milo, there is not an artist or scientist but would arrive immediately at the conclusion that there was originally a sculptor who conceived and carved the statue. The very lines and perfections would probably determine which of the great ancient artists carved the statue. Not only the unity of the Scriptures, but their lines of perfection, suggest One far above any human as the real author. That could be no one but God.[1]

Unity of Theme

There is certainly a unity of theme in the Bible: *Sinful humanity is redeemed by the grace of God.*

The story begins in Genesis with an account of the creation and fall of the race. Redemption was required by mankind's sinful rebellion against his Creator. This is related in the opening few chapters of the Bible. Redemption was then prepared for by means of God's promise to Abraham and the constitution of Israel as his chosen people through whom the Messiah and Savior would come. This narrative begins with Genesis 12 and continues through the historical section of the Old Testament. Redemption was then predicted through a series of poets and prophets who foretold the coming of the Messiah, his suffering for the sins of others, and the establishment of his kingdom.

Redemption becomes reality in Scripture through the events related in the Gospels, the first four books of the New Testament. They tell of the birth, life, death, and resurrection of Jesus of Nazareth and of his ascension to the right hand of God, where he sits on the throne of David in glory. Redemption is then proclaimed and shared by the apostles and prophets of the early church. The Book of Acts tells how the gospel was preached to the Jews first and then to the Gentiles as well. It pictures the rapid growth of the church and the reign of God among his people. Redemption is explained in terms of its practical implications in the Epistles (Romans through Jude) of the New Testament. Finally, redemption is realized in the Book of Revelation. The final book of the New Testament, Revelation assures the people of God that they will share in Christ's victory over the world and evil.

Unity of Structure

The foregoing brief survey of the Bible's unity of theme also displays a conspicuous *unity of structure* to Scripture:

The Old Testament is the New concealed, and the New Testament is the Old revealed.

There is a gap of roughly four hundred years between the last part of the Old Testament to be written and the earliest section of the New Testament produced. Yet the link between the close of the Old and opening of the New is obvious. Malachi closes the Old Testament with a prediction of the next major event on the divine schedule—the appearance of the Messiah and his herald: "'See, I will send my messenger, who will prepare the way before me. Then suddenly the Lord you are seeking will come to his temple, the messenger of the covenant, whom you desire, will come,' says the Lord Almighty" (Mal. 3:1; cf. 4:5–6).

Moving into the opening pages of the New Testament, one sees that the coming of John the Baptizer was regarded as the inception of the fulfillment of all the Old Testament expectations about the Messiah. Thus, the Gospel of Mark opens by referring to John's work as the "beginning of the gospel about Jesus Christ, the Son of God" (Mark 1:1). John told the people to repent because the long-awaited kingdom of God was at hand (cf. Matt. 3:1–3).

The Bible's structure resembles what a movie theater commonly does in advertising its coming attractions. The Old Testament closes with a preview of things to come so we would understand that the process of revelation was not finished. The New Testament is the sequel that brings the story to completion. Now we have a single assembly of divine revelation with every part fitting into its proper place in the structure of the whole.

This structural tie between the two testaments is further affirmed in the word *fulfilled* in the New Testament. "All this took place to fulfill what the Lord has said through the prophet . . ." (Matt. 1:22; cf. 2:5–6, 15, 17–18, 23; 3:3; 4:14, *et al.*). The early parts of the Bible were written in expectation of someone (Jesus) and something (the kingdom of heaven), both yet to come. The final parts were written in the confidence that all things were now accomplished.

Concerning this salvation, the prophets, who spoke of the grace that was to come to you, searched intently and with the greatest care, trying to find out the time and circumstances to which the Spirit of Christ in them was pointing when he predicted the sufferings of Christ and the glories that would follow. It was revealed to them that they were not serving themselves but you, when they spoke of the things that have now been told you by those who have preached the gospel to you by the Holy Spirit sent from heaven . . . (1 Peter 1:10–12).

Unity of Focus

Through all this, of course, the fundamental unity of Scripture is its *unity of focus: Jesus Christ.* Everything before his arrival anticipates him. Everything after his arrival reveals the meaning of his coming and its implications for our lives.

The Bible, though many parts, is one book. Each part is connected to every other part in theme, structure, and focus. Each part interprets and clarifies every other part. Each part contributes to the understanding of the whole. This sort of unity could not have come about by accident. It is an indisputable internal proof that the human writers of Scripture "spoke from God as they were carried along by the Holy Spirit" (2 Peter 1:21b).

Predictive Prophecy

The strongest single evidence of the Bible's divine origin, and the feature that underlies the unity just discussed, is predictive prophecy.

Biblical prophecies about future events are unique and striking phenomena. They cry out for an explanation. Although unbelievers have appealed to every conceivable device and argument to explain them away, the predictions and their fulfillments stand as clear matters of historical record. They are incontrovertible proof that the Bible is from God. How so? No man can make specific and detailed predictions of future events except by inspiration of God. Only someone who knows all things, including the end of all things from the beginning—that is, God—can predict the future with unfailing accuracy.

Every one of the scores of Old and New Testament predictive prophecies has been fulfilled to the letter, except for those relating to the second coming of Christ, the final judgment, and eternity. The fact of the fulfillment of those prior prophecies is conclusive proof to Christians that the remaining ones will also come to pass.

The Bible itself places great emphasis on predictive prophecy as proof of the integrity of the total system of things revealed therein. The following challenge, for example, was issued to the priests of the idol-gods of Babylon in the eighth century B.C.:

> "Present your case," says the LORD,
>   "Set forth your arguments," says Jacob's King.
> *"Bring in your idols to tell us*
>   *what is going to happen.*
> Tell us what the former things were,
>   so that we may consider them
>   and know their final outcome.
> *Or declare to us the things to come,*
>   *tell us what the future holds,*
>   *so we may know that you are gods"* (Isa. 41:21–23a, italics added).

While challenging the dumb idols of the pagans to do what was obviously outside their power, the ability of the God of Israel to predict the future is held out as a vindication of his reality, power, and veracity:

> "Remember the former things, those of long ago;
>   I am God, and there is no other;
>   I am God, and there is none like me.
> *I make known the end from the beginning,*
>   *from ancient times, what is still to come.*
> I say: My purpose will stand,
>   and I will do all that I please" (Isa. 46:9–10, italics added).

In the New Testament, all four Gospel writers appealed to the fulfillment of Old Testament predictions in the life and ministry of Jesus as proof of his messiahship. Matthew, the first and most thoroughly Jewish of the Gospels, quotes Hebrew Scripture extensively and presents Jesus in the light of the prediction-fulfillment motif. Using both direct and typological predictions, he argues his case based on the Scripture's anticipation of the Son of man.

Through the course of history, apologists for the Christian faith have used this same confirmation from predictive prophecy again and again. The second century is sometimes called the Age of the Apologists. Particularly during the period from about 130 to 180, there appeared several apologists who took up the task of defending the faith with reasoned proofs. Such men as Justin Martyr, Tatian of Syria, Athenagoras of Athens, and Theophilus of Antioch set themselves to the task of defending this new religion.

An example of the literature that survives from the second-century apologists is *The First Apology of Justin*, written around 155 and addressed to the Roman emperor Antoninus Pius. As with Matthew's Gospel, the theme of it is the messiahship of Jesus Christ. Following the pattern already established in the New Testament, Justin devoted primary attention to the argument from predictive prophecy. At the end of his argument, he writes:

> I could cite many other prophecies too, but pause, thinking that these are sufficient to convince those who have ears to hear and understand, and considering that such people can understand that we do not, like those who tell the mythical stories about the so-called sons of Zeus, merely talk, without having proofs.[2]

In chapter 10 of this book, we will explore an argument for the deity and messiahship of Jesus based on predictive prophecy. In this chapter, however, we shall deliberately steer away from the dozens of predictive prophecies about him, so as to establish a case for the divine inspiration of the Bible, a book that contains such marvelous instances of foreknowledge.

The basic meaning of the word *prophecy* is not prediction but the verbalization of the mind of God. It is the declaration of things one could not have known by ordinary means. Whether with regard to the past, present, or future, a prophet was someone who could reveal the mind of God toward the event or person in question.

To this point in the chapter, I have used the cumbersome term *predictive prophecy* to refer to the form of statement most of us think of as "prophetic." From this point forward, I will use the shorter and simpler term—prophecy—to refer only to those statements that involve foretelling the future.

Characteristics of Authentic Prophecies

To be a genuine prophecy, which can be appealed to for validation of divine involvement, a statement must satisfy three criteria.

First, the prophecy must deal with persons or events that are remote enough in time from the prediction that it cannot be mere conjecture or inference. Scientific predictions of eclipses or atmospheric events, for example, are not "prophetic" in the sense this criterion demands. Such forecasts are statements of confidence in nature's orderly functioning. They are based on observable data and logical inferences from that data. This criterion also requires that a prophecy be the foretelling of an event whose fulfillment the prophet could not have contrived. As a matter of fact, biblical prophecy will be shown to be of such a nature as to be not only generations removed from the prophet and his immediate influence, but also diametrically opposed to what human experience and reason would predict.

Second, the prophecy cannot be a matter of vague generalization that later could be applied to a situation in some questionable way. "There will be political turmoil in Egypt" hardly qualifies as a prophecy of specific content.

Whether the words were spoken three thousand years ago or today, some event has taken place or will occur that could be claimed as their fulfillment. With biblical prophecies, people are named and their destinies traced long before they are even born. Nations are characterized before they exist, and wars are described before they are fought. The more detailed the prophecy and the more unusual its nature, of course, the greater its evidential nature. While it must be admitted that some prophecies in the Bible are less specific than others, the biblical predictions are anything but obscure.

Third, the prophecy's fulfillment must be unmistakable and clear. After all, mere prediction is no evidence of supernatural presence and power. It is the clear fulfillment of the prediction in an unmistakable manner that proves its divine character.

Some Examples of Biblical Prophecy

As examples of the type of prophecies found in the Bible, there are several relating to the fate of cities and nations of antiquity.

In the heyday of "Babylon," Isaiah prophesied of its total desolation. That wealthy and powerful city was surrounded by a wall wide enough for three chariots to be driven abreast on its top. Its hanging gardens were one of the seven wonders of the ancient world. It had paved streets, running water, and many of the conveniences we associate only with modern cities.

In the eighth century B.C., Isaiah claimed to receive this message from God:

> See, I will stir up against them the Medes,
>> who do not care for silver
>> and have no delight in gold.
> Their bows will strike down the young men;
>> they will have no mercy on infants
>> nor will they look with compassion on children.
> Babylon, the jewel of kingdoms,
>> the glory of the Babylonians' pride,

will be overthrown by God
   like Sodom and Gomorrah.
She will never be inhabited
   or lived in through all generations;
no Arab will pitch his tent there,
   no shepherd will rest his flocks there.
But desert creatures will lie there,
   jackals will fill her houses;
there the owls will dwell,
   and there the wild goats will leap about.
Hyenas will howl in her strongholds,
   jackals in her luxurious palaces.
Her time is at hand,
   and her days will not be prolonged (Isa. 13:17–22).

The people who initially heard or read this prediction must have thought Isaiah was a madman. How could the world's richest and most distinguished city become totally desolated? Oh, of course, one might predict its future defeat at the hands of an enemy and might even be lucky enough to name the enemy correctly. But desolated? Abandoned? Uninhabited? For two millennia now, history has stood as incontestable proof that Isaiah's information was reliable.

The Medes came against Babylon in 539 B.C. and, under the leadership of Cyrus, conquered it. Its destruction was made complete when Cyrus's son-in-law, Xerxes, later plundered the city. Its desolation was so complete that, when Alexander the Great later decided to repopulate and restore it, he gave up the task as a hopeless one.

Against ancient "Tyre," Ezekiel gave this prophecy:

. . . this is what the Sovereign LORD says: I am against you, O Tyre, and I will bring many nations against you, like the sea casting up its waves. They will destroy the walls of Tyre and pull down her towers; I will scrape away her rubble and make her a bare rock. Out in the sea she will become a place to spread fishnets, for I have spoken, declares the Sovereign LORD. She will become plunder for the nations.

. . . I will make you a bare rock, and you will become a
place to spread fishnets. You will never be rebuilt, for I the
LORD have spoken, declares the Sovereign LORD (Ezek.
26:3–5, 14).

Given around 588 B.C., this prediction speaks of
Yahweh's coming wrath against the capital city of the
Phoenician Empire. Its essential points for our purpose
here include that Tyre would have "many nations" rise
against her (v. 3), be so dismantled as to be left a "bare
rock" (vs. 4, 14), and serve as "a place to spread fishnets"
(v. 14).

From 587–574 B.C., Nebuchadnezzar led a siege against
the proud city of Tyre. The mainland city was overrun as a
result, and the people of Tyre fled to an island about one-
half mile offshore in the Mediterranean Sea. There the city
existed until 332 B.C. In that year Alexander the Great came
against it and, in a most ingenious manner, overcame the
problem that had stalled Nebuchadnezzar and the
Babylonian armies. Alexander tore down the ruins of the
old mainland city and used its stones, timbers, and topsoil
to construct a land bridge over to the island. Even this,
however, was in fulfillment of divine prophecy. Ezekiel
had said of Tyre's enemies: "They will break down your
walls and demolish your fine houses and throw your
stones, timber and rubble into the sea" (Ezek. 26:12b).

When Alexander died and his empire began to be
carved up by his generals, Antigonus came against Tyre
yet again in 314 B.C. and plundered it once more. Today,
the site of the old mainland city is nothing more than a
barren rock where fishermen can be seen spreading their
nets.

Many nations. Devastated. Left a "bare rock" and never
rebuilt. Used for the spreading of nets. How could Ezekiel
have known all those things so far in advance of their fulfillment? He couldn't have known. *But God did!* And
through the prophet Ezekiel, he foretold them. Now the
record of the predictions and their exact fulfillments stand

as an invitation for all people to recognize the book containing them as the very Word of God to the human family.

The fate of "Nineveh" was also foretold accurately through the prophets of God. Roughly a century and a half after Nineveh had been visited by Jonah, heard his message of impending destruction, repented, and was spared, the city's sinfulness again became so great that the Spirit of God moved the prophets Nahum and Zephaniah to speak against it.

> [God] will stretch out his hand against the north
>   and destroy Assyria,
> leaving Nineveh utterly desolate
>   and dry as the desert.
> Flocks and herds will lie down there,
>   creatures of every kind.
> The desert owl and the screech owl
>   will roost on her columns.
> Their calls will echo through the windows,
>   rubble will be in the doorways,
>   the beams of cedar will be exposed.
> This is the carefree city
>   that lived in safety.
> She said to herself,
>   "I am, and there is none besides me."
> What a ruin she has become,
>   a lair for wild beasts!
> All who pass by her scoff
>   and shake their fists (Zeph. 2:13–15; cf. Nah. 1:1–8).

In 612 B.C., the combined forces of the Babylonians and Medes came against Nineveh and completely destroyed it. The once proud and powerful city was in ruins and had become an object of derision. The word of a Spirit-guided prophet had been fulfilled again.

Were prophecies such as these against Babylon, Tyre, and Nineveh just the recorded ravings of men who were jealous of their grandeur? Did it just coincidentally turn out that their predictions came true? If the prophecies were few and far between, perhaps that explanation would be credible. If some of their predictions came to pass and others failed, perhaps that theory would be justified. But the fulfillment of every one of the scores of prophecies found in Scripture points to a supernatural origin. It is the only explanation that fits the facts.

The major objection that could be offered against this argument for inspiration based on predictive prophecies is to insist that the alleged prophecies were written *after* the events they pretend to foretell. It is certainly true that ancient documents are sometimes difficult to date and that the dating of biblical materials is not absolutely certain in many cases. But the arbitrary assignment of dates after the major prophetic events in the document is an act of prejudice based on the assumption of antisupernaturalism. It betrays an *a priori* belief that rules out the possibility of prophecy occurring and forces one to date the text after the events in question.

It is easy enough to show, however, that even when the latest possible dates are granted for all the Old Testament materials, there remains a large enough body of prophecies to establish a conclusive case for the claim of inspiration. The Old Testament predictions about Jesus of Nazareth, for example, were certainly not written after he fulfilled them.

Anticipations of Modern Science

Although some people uncritically consider modern science an enemy of faith, science actually testifies eloquently to the supernatural origin of the Bible. In spite of the fact that its various parts were written centuries ago, there is an amazing treatment of science in the Bible that transcends human invention and the knowledge of the period in which it was produced. Beyond that, it anticipates many of the discoveries of science by hundreds of years.

The preoccupation of our generation with the marvels of science has caused some people to attempt to make too great an issue of the Bible's science and pre-science. Some have even claimed to find the atomic bomb, color TV, and space travel in the Bible. May we be spared such absurd claims!

The Bible is remarkable, though, for the things it does *not* say about our world and life within it. For example, the ancient Egyptians believed our planet was supported on five great pillars. Although Moses was brought up in Egyptian court circles and "educated in all the wisdom of the Egyptians" (Acts 7:22), one searches in vain for any trace of such an unscientific notion in his writings. The notions of a flat Earth, spontaneous generation of life, Ptolemaic astronomy, and countless other commonly accepted but unscientific errors of ancient times are noticeably absent from Scripture.

The famous *Papyrus Ebers*, a medical book written in Egypt around the time of Moses, contains prescriptions such as this one: "To prevent the hair from turning gray, anoint it with the blood of a black calf which has been boiled in oil, or with the fat of a rattlesnake."[3] Victims of poisonous snake bites were treated with "magic water," produced by pouring water over an idol. Embedded splinters were treated with worms' blood and asses' dung—a sure way to bolster the likelihood of death by lockjaw, since animal dung is loaded with tetanus spores.

In contrast, the amazing character of certain Old Testament instructions about hygiene, sanitation, and quarantine of infectious disease are unique in ancient literature and anticipated many modern discoveries. For example, the requirement to ancient Israel that human waste be buried outside the people's desert camp (cf. Deut. 23:12–13) would have had an obvious health advantage to them. And there are some remarkable passages on the diagnosis and prevention of leprosy in Leviticus 13. One scholar observes: "This material is all the more significant because its technical nature attests to its antiquity, and also because it comprises the first formulation of the principles of quarantine and preventive medicine as applied to leprosy to be recovered from the culture of the ancient Near East."[4]

There can be no doubt that the medical practices of the Jews of Moses' time were significantly advanced beyond those of surrounding nations. While one must remember that these rules and regulations were given to them in a religious context as tests of faith, the fact remains that they reflect scientifically accurate principles and procedures.

> It is entirely immaterial whether the hygiene and prophylaxis as promulgated by Moses in the Pentateuch were intended as religious rituals or as health measures. The fact is they were scientifically sound. . . . The fact is that neither the Old Egyptian medical documents nor other early medical codes have been so thoroughgoing on subjects of hygiene and prophylaxis as the Mosaic Code.[5]

The Bible is not a "child of its times," as some detractors would say. It is not marred by the crude and backward ideas of ancient scientists. And the only possible explanation for this phenomenon is that its content came from God rather than mere men.

Conclusion

The Bible is the freshest and most perpetually relevant book in the history of the world. Textbooks on science are frequently outdated before they come from the press. Volumes on history have to be revised because of new information that comes to light. Encyclopedias have to be rewritten constantly because human knowledge is increasing at such a phenomenal rate. But the Bible never becomes antiquated.

Read the Old Testament prophets and you will think they are describing people in our own generation. No suffering person can express the innermost feelings of his or her own heart so well as they are expressed in Psalms. The

Gospels, showing us the incomparable Christ, have lost nothing of their vibrant challenge with the passing of time.

We humans have never been able to lift ourselves by our own bootstraps, but the Bible has uplifted us immeasurably. Mortals have never been able to chart a secure course through the fog of disappointments and heartaches in human affairs, but the Bible is our compass, guiding us toward a safe harbor. Just by virtue of its dynamic impact on human lives, one can know that the Bible is more than *a* book. It is *the* Book of books. It is the inspired Word of God.

The American Bible Society once conducted an interesting experiment in Chicago. They chose a five-block area in a district with one of the highest crime rates in the city and flooded it with seven thousand copies of the Gospel of John. They included an invitation for anyone who wanted more reading material to send for a copy of the complete New Testament. They received around two hundred requests. The district police captain later reported that the crime rate in the area dropped dramatically in one month's time. The same experiment produced similar results in another area with a high crime rate.

Wherever the Bible has gone, it has had a profound impact on people's lives. Recognizing that unique influence on the formation and development of the United States of America, Congress requested that President Reagan proclaim 1983 as the Year of the Bible. In his proclamation, he encouraged all citizens of the country "to re-examine and rediscover [the Bible's] priceless and timeless message."

Far from being an ancient millstone around the necks of modern men and women, the Bible is God's Word for all people of all times and cultures. It provides the only dependable knowledge we can have about the mind of God.

The Bible speaks to our deepest needs. We feel guilt, and the Bible points to forgiveness through Jesus. We face tragedy and death, and the Bible shows us that God cares about us in every life situation and that death has been conquered through the Son of God. It provides guidance for our lives by revealing where we came from, to whom we are responsible, and what is necessary to live an abundant life.

7

Some Facts About the Bible

The point of the two previous chapters has been to argue that the Bible, as originally given through men in its various parts, was a gift from God and therefore true, complete, and authoritative. These men were not left to give their own opinions or mere personal feelings about matters discussed in Scripture; they were fully borne along by the Holy Spirit so that every word they wrote was a God-breathed word.

But even if this is granted about Scripture *as it was originally given* (the autographs), what confidence do we have that its ancient content has not been lost or altered in the long process of transmission and translation through which the English Bible has come into our hands? Are there books other than the sixty-six in our present canon that should be included in the Bible? Can we know that we possess the original message God gave to us through the apostles and prophets?

It is to these problems that we turn our attention in this chapter.

The Providence of God

When one first begins to reflect on the matter of transmission and translation of Scripture, an obvious presupposition quickly comes to mind: *If the original manuscripts of the various biblical books were brought into being as the result of the workings of Almighty God, surely that same God has seen to the providential preservation of their contents through the ages.* Heaven's work of communication—designed to bring lost humanity to salvation—would have been an imperfect work if the process were not overseen and brought to a successful end. It is rather absurd to suppose that God would go to the great lengths he did for the original writing down of his will for humanity and then abandon the process of revelation so that no assurance is possible for generations of mankind far removed from the original writing of the Scripture.

The most ancient parts of Scripture are thirty-five hundred years old; the most recent parts are around nineteen hundred years old. Though written on such perishable substances as clay tablets, cured animal skins, and papyrus, and having to be copied by hand for hundreds of years before the invention of printing, the Bible has not only survived but has survived against staggering odds. For example, the Roman emperor Diocletian issued an edict in 303 requiring the destruction of all church buildings, the burning of all the sacred writings of the Christians, and the denial of civil rights to all citizens of the empire who persisted in embracing the religion of Jesus Christ. He was determined to stamp out Christianity by destroying the Bible.

Through the centuries, Diocletian has had many heirs who were bent on destroying either the Bible itself or people's confidence in the Bible as God's Word. They have all failed. Thus, while many other important writings of antiquity have been totally lost to us through benign neglect, the Bible has survived determined efforts to destroy it.

Furthermore, Scripture has survived with such a wealth of evidence that the authenticity of its texts is not open to serious question. Yet the charge is still heard occasionally that we have only a spurious Bible in our possession. It takes something of the following form: "The Bible has been tampered with and changed so often through the centuries that nobody really knows what was in its original text."

The claim that we *do* have the text of the Bible faithfully preserved for us does not rest merely upon the sort of presupposition mentioned above. An important field of biblical study called "textual criticism" concerns itself with meticulous investigations into the reliability of the text of the Bible. Let us turn to an examination of some of the data provided us by the textual critics.

Concerning the Old Testament

There are no original manuscripts, or autographs, of any Old Testament books available to the students of the sacred text. Yet, from what has been learned about the painstaking copying and preservation of books at the hands of Jewish professionals, there is every reason to have confidence in the Old Testament that has been preserved for us.

During the period from approximately 300 B.C. to A.D. 500, the duty of preserving and transmitting the Hebrew Bible fell to the ancient scribes or *Sopherim*. These men took extreme care to preserve the text in as pure a form as possible, including the counting of the words and letters in each book. They counted to the middle word and middle letter of each book, calculated how many times a letter was used in each book, and compiled other statistics that reduced the possibility of copying errors creeping into their scrolls.

The work of the scribes ended around A.D. 500, and in their place arose the Massoretes, about whom it is said:

> The Massoretes were the custodians of the sacred traditional text, and were active from about A.D. 500 to 1000. They continued and completed the objectives of the *Sopherim* and the rabbis by definitely fixing a form of the Hebrew text, which subsequently became known as Massoretic. Accordingly they concerned themselves with the transmission of the consonantal text as they had received it, as well as with its pronunciation, on the basis that the text itself was inviolable and every consonant sacred.[1]

All this attests that Scripture was afforded the greatest reverence by its custodians. Every possible precaution was taken to assure the purity of the sacred text. The copying of Old Testament manuscripts was no haphazard thing, to be regarded with disdain by modern man. To the contrary, it was a far more meticulous thing than today's humans are willing to undertake in our typical impatience and haste.

An indication of the sacredness of the biblical text to the Jewish people is found in Josephus, the Jewish historian who wrote for the Romans. Although a melodramatic statement in form, which surely overstates the degree of devotion the Romans had for their own sacred writings, it nonetheless affirms the determination to keep the documents inviolable:

> We have given practical proof of our reverence for our own Scriptures. For, although such long ages have now passed, no one has ventured either to add, or to remove, or to alter a syllable; and it is an instinct with every Jew, from the day of his birth, to regard them as the decrees of God, to abide by them, and, if need be, cheerfully to die for them.[2]

We are still left with the question, however, about how well the process actually worked. Does the Massoretic Text faithfully represent the Hebrew Bible as originally given and as known, for example, by Jesus and his apostles? A series of events dating from 1947 enables us to answer this question with conviction.

Before that, the oldest extensive manuscript of any Old Testament book known to us was from around A.D. 900. In 1947, a discovery was made in a cave near the northwestern edge of the Dead Sea that has been far-reaching in its consequences. The Qumran caves have yielded biblical manuscripts from every book in the Old Testament except Esther, and discoveries are still being made.

These documents survive from a Jewish religious sect that had established a separate community in the Judean desert from about 150 B.C. until sometime in the seventh decade of the Christian era. The people living in this little community spent much of their time studying and copying Scripture. When it became apparent to them that their land was going to be overrun by the Romans, they put their precious scrolls in earthenware jars and buried them in a series of caves near the Dead Sea. Following the destruction of Jerusalem, the former inhabitants of the little community never returned, and their library of manuscripts went undetected until 1947.

On one account of their discovery, a fifteen-year-old Bedouin boy stumbled onto the documents quite by accident. As he threw a stone at a fugitive goat, it struck a pottery jar. The boy traced the sound to its origin and found several other jars inside a cave, which had been sealed over for centuries. When scholars examined what he had found, they were dumbfounded. Other manuscripts were found in the original cave, and several other manuscript-bearing caves were eventually discovered.

The significance of the Dead Sea Scrolls is their testimony to the accuracy of transmission of the Old Testament. The scrolls of Qumran were roughly a thousand years older than any of the manuscripts that Old Testament scholars had been working with before their discovery. By a careful comparison of the Dead Sea Scrolls with the Massoretic Text [M.T.], textual critics could now get a clear indication of the accuracy of transmission of the Old Testament over a period of a millennium. What was revealed by such a study?

> For example, we may study the copy b of Isaiah. The text is extremely close to our M.T. A comparison of Isaiah 53 shows that only seventeen letters differ from the M.T. Ten of these are mere differences in spelling, like "honor" or "honour," and make no change at all in meaning. Four more are very minor differences such as the presence of the conjunction which is often a matter of style. The other three letters are the Hebrew word for "light" which is added

after "they shall see" in verse 11. Out of 166 words in this
chapter only this one word is really in question and it does
not at all change the sense of the passage.

This is typical of the whole manuscript. Even the use of
vowel letters and the preservation of archaic grammatical
forms are exceedingly close to the M.T.[3]

Of the Dead Sea Scrolls and their testimony to the accuracy of transmission of the Old Testament, Gleason L.
Archer has written:

Even though the two copies of Isaiah discovered in
Qumran Cave 1 near the Dead Sea in 1947 were a thousand
years earlier than the oldest dated manuscript previously
known (A.D. 980), they proved to be word for word identical with our standard Hebrew Bible in more than 95 per
cent of the text. The 5 per cent of variation consisted chiefly
of obvious slips of the pen and variations in spelling.[4]

Besides the valuable manuscripts of various Old
Testament books, there are also some other important
sources that the textual critic can use in determining the
original text of the Hebrew Bible. These sources consist of
various versions, or translations, of the Old Testament. The
most important of these versions is the *Septuagint*, a translation of the entire Old Testament into the Greek language.
This version was begun around 250 B.C. and was the Bible
of the earliest Christians. Luke especially reflects the
Septuagint in his writings.

A rather free translation of the Old Testament into
Aramaic is known as a *targum*. Such translations were
made necessary after the Babylonian Captivity, when
Aramaic replaced Hebrew as the language of the Jews.
These were first done only orally and were finally commit-
ted to writing several centuries after the time of Christ.
Several targums exist, and some are of greater value than
others in reflecting the Hebrew text with accuracy. There
are also some Syriac, Latin, and Greek (other than the
Septuagint) versions known to the textual critics.

All the evidence available to the Old Testament textual critic points to the conclusion that the text of the Hebrew Bible has been preserved with an amazing care and accuracy. Confident that the very words of the book were from God, meticulous care was taken by its custodians as they preserved it for future generations. H. H. Rowley has written: "We may rest assured that the consonantal text of the Hebrew Bible, though not infallible, has been preserved with an accuracy perhaps unparalleled in any other Near-Eastern literature."[5]

Concerning the New Testament

As with the original copies of the Old Testament books, there are no original copies of the letters of Paul or the Gospels available for our handling and reading today.

It is true that we do not possess any of the original manuscripts. Perhaps this is just as well, since the history of Christianity has shown a tendency to worship ancient relics. But this does not mean that we are any less certain about the original text. This writer is not aware that we have the original text (called autographs) of any important ancient document. But if an original was widely circulated early, was copied, was quoted, and was translated into different languages, it can be reconstructed by a comparison of the different witnesses. Actually, if only one witness had been kept by itself, that one source might have been stolen and replaced by a substitute, whereas many independent witnesses, even if they are secondary, cannot be fabricated.[6]

A wealth of manuscript evidence is available to the textual critic in his study of the New Testament documents. Bruce M. Metzger[7] is a recognized authority in this field and informs us that there are roughly five thousand Greek manuscripts available to the textual critic that contain all or part of the New Testament.

Perhaps we can appreciate how wealthy the New Testament is in manuscript attestation if we compare the textual material for other ancient historical works. For Caesar's *Gallic War* (composed between 58 and 50 BC) there are several extant MSS [manuscripts], but only nine or ten are good, and the oldest is some 900 years later than Caesar's day. Of the 142 books of the Roman History of Livy (59 BC–AD 17) only thirty-five survive; these are known to us from not more than twenty MSS of any consequence, only one of which, and that containing fragments of Books iii–vi, is as old as the fourth century. . . . The History of Thucydides (*c.* 460–400 BC) is known to us from eight MSS, the earliest belonging to *c.* AD 900, and a few papyrus scraps, belonging to about the beginning of the Christian era. The same is true of the History of Herodotus (*c.* 480–425 BC). Yet no classical scholar would listen to an argument that the authenticity of Herodotus is in doubt because the earliest MSS of their works which are of any use to us are over 1,300 years later than the originals.[8]

The oldest and most important manuscripts of the New Testament known to us are written entirely in capital letters and are called *uncials*. There are approximately three hundred of these available to textual critics. The oldest and best of all the uncials are the Vatican Manuscript (kept in the Vatican Library at Rome), the Sinaitic Manuscript (found in a monastery on Mt. Sinai), and the Alexandrian Manuscript (first known to modern scholars from Alexandria, Egypt). These are all written on vellum and date from A.D. 300–450.

The next oldest manuscripts are those written in a smaller, running hand. Named for the style of writing employed in producing them, they are known as *cursives*. These all date from the ninth to the fifteenth centuries and number more than twenty-five hundred.

The very oldest materials of the New Testament text available to scholars are in the form of *papyrus fragments*. Because papyrus deteriorates in other climates, such fragments have been found only in Egypt. Although in some ways inferior to the uncial manuscripts mentioned above (due to the fact that they are not as complete), there is a sense in which they are superior to the uncials because they bear witness to the existence of New Testament materials at a very early date. For example, certain liberal scholars had argued that the Gospel of John was not written until the middle of the second century. But the John Rylands Fragment (P^{52}), containing a few verses from John's Gospel (John 19:31–33, 37, 38), is confidently dated within the first half of the second century and shows conclusively that a copy of the book was being circulated in Egypt within only a few years after it was written. This papyrus fragment is our oldest known piece of New Testament manuscript.

The Chester Beatty Papyri were found and published in the 1930s. These are the remains of three ancient collections of New Testament documents. The first group contains materials from the four Gospels and Acts and is designated P^{45}. The second group (P^{46}) is a large collection of the epistles of Paul. The third group (P^{47}) contains the text of Revelation 9–17. The Beatty Papyri date from the third century.

Within the last few years, the Bodmer Library of Geneva published an entire copy of the Gospel of John (P^{66}) that dates from about A.D. 200. The importance of this document is readily apparent. The same source has also published the earliest known copies of Jude and the epistles of Peter (P^{72}), dating from the third century. The entire text of the Gospels of Luke and John, dating from between A.D. 175 and 225, have also been published by the Bodmer Library (P^{75}).

All the evidence available to biblical scholars confirms the reliability of the text available to students of the Word of God. Sir Frederic Kenyon, director of the British Museum for twenty-one years and an eminent scholar in this field, has said:

> The interval then between the dates of original composition and the earliest extant evidence becomes so small as to be in fact negligible, as the last foundation for any doubt that

the Scriptures have come down to us substantially as they were written has now been removed. Both the authenticity and the general integrity of the books of the New Testament may be regarded as finally established.[9]

Aside from the manuscripts already mentioned, there are three other important sources of information that add to our assurance that the New Testament books have been faithfully transmitted through the ages.

First, there are the versions. Very early in its history, the New Testament began to be translated into various languages for the sake of missionary work. Since these translations were made so early and from Greek manuscripts very near the autographs in point of time, they are helpful to the textual critic in dealing with certain matters of importance. The three groups of translations of greatest significance are the Syriac versions, the Coptic (or Egyptian) versions, and the Latin versions. J. W. Roberts comments:

> There are problems in reconstructing the text from translations. Admittedly many idioms cannot be translated. But for checking the absence or presence of a given reading in the text being used by the translators, these versions are especially helpful. There is no portion of the Greek New Testament which cannot be checked "from the mouth of two or three witnesses" by these three translations.[10]

Second, there is the valuable body of writings from the church fathers. These men wrote from the period at the end of the first century and shortly afterward. Although the fathers were certainly not empowered as the apostles before them had been, they possessed copies of the inspired Scripture that, of course, were older than the manuscripts now remaining to us. Since their writings treated topics of interest and controversy among the earliest believers, they naturally quoted many Scripture texts in the course of their discussions. Some scholars assert that the entire text of the New Testament could be recovered from the multitude of Scripture quotations contained in the writings of the fathers.

Third, there is the evidence provided by the lectionaries: "The term *lection* refers to a selected passage of Scripture designed to be read in the public worship services, and thus a lectionary is a manuscript especially arranged in sections for this purpose."[11] As one would expect, most lectionaries are composed from the Gospels. A good many, however, contain readings from Acts and the New Testament Epistles. Even though they do not date before the sixth century, the texts from which they quote were certainly older, and they were evidently copied very carefully since they were intended for use in public worship. More than eighteen hundred lectionaries are known to scholars of the biblical text, and they constitute a textual witness of significant value.

Thus, we can be confident of having more than adequate evidence to establish the fact that we have a trustworthy text of both the Old and New Testaments. The sixty-six books contained in the Bible constitute the complete body of inspired literature known to mankind today and are "useful for teaching, rebuking, correcting and training in righteousness, so that the man of God may be thoroughly equipped for every good work" (2 Tim. 3:16–17).

People sometimes ask why it is that the Catholic Bible contains more books than the sixty-six generally recognized as canonical. These "apocryphal" books do not claim to be the Word of God, are obviously inferior in content and value to the canonical books, and were never accepted as God-breathed literature by either the Jews or the earliest Christians. No one need fear that our Bibles with sixty-six books are lacking or incomplete.

A Word About the Canon

Our English word *canon* comes from a Greek term meaning rod or ruler, a straight-edged tool used for determining the straightness of an object. The word eventually came to be applied to the accepted books that constitute a rule of faith for Christians. First used this way about three hundred years after the time of Christ, the term "canon of Scripture" denotes the list or catalog of writings received as God-breathed and authoritative.

Canonization was not a formal process that took place when a group of church officials met to decide which writings to include and which to exclude from the Bible. As books that bore the marks of inspiration were written, they were immediately treated with respect and regarded as authoritative. Copies were made and shared with other groups of believers, and collections of sacred writings began to accumulate. Among the Jews with their manuscripts and with the Christians later, the idea of a canon existed long before a term was adopted to express it.

Old Testament

According to the Talmud, the Jews used the phrase "defile the hands" from the first century A.D. forward to identify writings suitable for reading in the synagogue. When the Torah had been produced through Moses, for example, there was no need for someone to pronounce it canonical. As Moses had been the undisputed leader of the nation of Israel and the one through whom God revealed himself to the people, the materials he wrote down were immediately regarded as inspired, obligatory, and unalterable.

As other materials came to be written within the community of Israel, acceptance grew out of their concurrence with the Mosaic writings and from the personal authentication the writers received through signs given by God during their ministries. The process by which the Old Testament canon took form was thus a gradual and extended one over a considerable period of time.

Early on in the process, the Jews apportioned the Old Testament writings into a tripartite division of Law, Prophets, and Writings. The Law (Torah or Pentateuch) included the five books of Moses—Genesis, Exodus, Leviticus, Numbers, Deuteronomy—which were called "the five-fifths of the Law." The Prophets incorporated the four so-called Former Prophets (Joshua, Judges, 1 and 2 Samuel [counted as one book], and 1 and 2 Kings [counted as one book]), the four so-called Latter Prophets (Isaiah, Jeremiah, Ezekiel, and the Twelve Minor Prophets of Hosea through Malachi [counted as a single book])—a total of eight books. The Writings embraced the eleven books of Psalms, Proverbs, Job, Song of Solomon, Ruth, Lamentations, Ecclesiastes, Esther, Daniel, Ezra-Nehemiah (counted as one book) and 1 and 2 Chronicles (counted as one book).

This threefold canon has twenty-four books on the basis of the customary Hebrew division of the materials. By the way we divide the same materials, the Christian canon counts thirty-nine books for the Old Testament.

The process of standardization of accepted books had certainly been completed before the time of Jesus and the writing of the New Testament. Thus, the New Testament can speak of "Scripture(s)" (Matt. 22:29; John 10:35; 19:36; Acts 18:24; Rom. 1:2; 2 Peter 1:20), "sacred writings" (2 Tim. 3:15 NASB), or "Law and Prophets" (Matt. 5:17; 7:12; 22:40; Luke 16:16; Acts 13:15; 28:23). Jesus himself made explicit reference to the tripartite division of the Old Testament in speaking of matters "written about me in the Law of Moses, the Prophets and the Psalms" (Luke 24:44).

When the church was born from the womb of Judaism, it accepted the Jewish canon in its entirety. Thus, the content of the Hebrew Bible and the Christian Old Testament are the same except for the method of grouping materials into twenty-four and thirty-nine books respectively.

The Bible of the Roman Catholic Church contains more Old Testament material than the books just identified. Specifically, there are seven books (Tobit, Judith, Wisdom, Sirach, Baruch, 1 and 2 Maccabees), additions to Esther (10:4–16:24), and additions to Daniel (Song of the Three Holy Children inserted at 3:24–90; Susanna inserted as ch.

13; Bel and the Dragon inserted as ch. 14). These additions are advocated based on a so-called "larger canon" represented in the Septuagint.

Protestants reject these books, calling them "apocryphal," because the Jews have never included them in their Hebrew canon at any time or at any place. Furthermore, in the copies of the Septuagint that survive to us, the number and names of the additional books vary greatly. It is likely that the apocryphal books got into the Septuagint, traditionally held to have been produced at the instigation of Ptolemy Philadelphus (285–247 B.C.) of Egypt, because Ptolemy's interest was building up the library of Alexandria rather than representing or defining the Hebrew canon.

New Testament

The case of the New Testament canon is a bit different and developed over a shorter period of time. For one thing, the New Testament materials were written over a shorter time span. Beginning with the epistle of James (*ca.* A.D. 45) and ending with the Revelation (*ca.* A.D. 95), the twenty-seven units of the New Testament were produced over a half century of time rather than the Old Testament's eleven hundred years. For another, its canon appears to have developed almost "naturally"—without any sense of urgency to define it—until a crisis situation called forth a summary statement of what was already generally accepted within the believing community.

Colossians 4:16 seems to assume a practice of sharing, and possibly copying and collecting, letters of the apostles. Peter speaks, for example, of how Paul writes "in *all* his letters" with a wisdom God provided him (2 Peter 3:16). This may suggest the existence of a Pauline corpus well before the end of the first century. What we are certain about is that there was a general circulation of Paul's letters in the early second century and a tendency to quote from the Gospels as "Scripture."

Ironically, though, the first actual list of canonical New

Testament books known to us is from a second-century heretic named Marcion. Somewhere around A.D. 140, this man—who wanted to distinguish the God of the Old Testament from the God of the New Testament—published a two-part canon of "gospel" and "apostle." In the first category, he accepted a purged and edited version of Luke. In the second, he recognized ten of Paul's thirteen epistles, omitting 1 and 2 Timothy and Titus. The interesting thing about this one-man judgment about the canon is that it was a reduction and paring down of the books known to Christians in general.

Around 170, a scholar named Tatian published the *Diatessaron*. Meaning "through the four," this early harmony of the Gospels uses all four Gospels in our New Testament. He rejects other so-called Gospels in circulation at the time (some of which survive to us) in favor of the four we still accept as authoritative.

Irenaeus (*ca.* 180), in his *Against Heresies*, recognized the four Gospels, Acts, Paul's thirteen epistles, 1 Peter, 1 and 2 John, Revelation, and the Shepherd of Hermas.

We owe a great deal to Origen of Alexandria (*ca.* 230) for his discussion of the canon known to him. He identifies three classes of books: accepted, disputed, and false. The "accepted" materials were the four Gospels, thirteen Pauline epistles, 1 Peter, 1 John, Acts, and Revelation. The "disputed" were 2 Peter, 2 and 3 John, Hebrews, James, Jude, the Shepherd of Hermas, the epistle of Barnabas, and the Didache. The "false" were the Gospels in circulation other than Matthew, Mark, Luke, and John.

Eusebius of Caesarea (*ca.* 230) wrote his famous *Church History* and discussed the canon in terms of Origen's three categories identified above. His accepted books include the same ones Origen named and Hebrews. His disputed works he further subdivided into those "accepted by the majority" and others generally regarded as "spurious." The former were James, Jude, 2 Peter, and 2 and 3 John; the latter were the Didache, the epistle of Barnabas, and the Shepherd of Hermas.

Two significant dates in the history of the New Testament canon are 367 and 397. In 367, Athenasius of Alexandria wrote an Easter letter to the churches in which he lists the exact twenty-seven books we now recognize as canonical. Insofar as we know, the letter is the first use of the word *canonical* to describe this catalog of works. In 397, at the Third Council of Carthage, the same list of twenty-seven books was deemed "canonical" and appropriate for reading in the church's assemblies. This is the first statement on the canon from a general council of church leaders, with Augustine among them. It should be observed, however, that the council's action was not to decide the canon but to further endorse what had already developed as a consensus among the believers.

Late in his life, when Jerome (*ca.* 340–420) produced the Latin version of Scripture known as the Vulgate, the New Testament included the same books we have in our New Testaments today. Thus, we may say that the canon was fully formed, generally recognized, and consistently employed by A.D. 400.

As to the *tests of canonicity* employed in the discussions from the first century through the fourth, there was eventually only one—inspiration. Was the Holy Spirit its ultimate Author? Was it from God? This critical issue of inspiration seems to have boiled down to three tests.

The first was its relationship to an apostle. Was it written by an apostle (Matthew, John) or a close associate of an apostle (Mark's association with Peter, Luke's with Paul)? The reason that Hebrews was debated for inclusion in the canon was focused on this issue.

The second was its contents. Are its contents spiritual? On a par with the Old Testament and other recognized books? Appropriate for reading and encouragement in the churches? This test quickly and decisively eliminated most of the apocryphal materials that floated around during the early centuries.

The third test was universality. Was the book received widely among orthodox churches? This test served to eliminate Gospels and epistles written by heretical groups in an effort to legitimate some aberrant idea.

The Work of Translation

Finally, a word needs to be said in this chapter about the work of translation. Granted, we have dependable manuscripts of the Hebrew and Aramaic Old Testament and the Greek New Testament, but not many people are able to read these difficult languages. Most have to depend on translations from the Hebrew, Aramaic, and Greek manuscripts into their own native tongue. Might not something have been lost in the process? How can we be sure that we really have the Word of God in English?

To be sure, Bible translating is a human and uninspired enterprise. There is no such thing as an "inspired translation." The terms *inspired* and *infallible* belong only to the autographs of the biblical documents. Because translation of the Bible is a human process performed without the sort of divine intervention involved in giving the original text, there is no version of Scripture in any language that is above criticism. On the other hand, one can take comfort in the knowledge that there is no standard version so imperfect that an honest and inquiring person could not learn the story of redemption that unfolds in its pages.

The most trustworthy of the translations are what are usually called "standard translations." These have special merit due to the fact that they have been produced by large translation committees composed of scholars from various backgrounds and religious affiliations. Such authorities do their work within the guidelines of accepted translation procedures and check each other's work as it goes along. This system minimizes the possibility of one person's reading something into the text that is not actually there; it reduces the likelihood of having the translation "slanted" toward the translator's theological view; it encourages a faithful translation of the actual Hebrew, Aramaic, or Greek text without misrepresentation.

The most widely known and used of the standard

English translations in the United States are the King
James Version (including the New King James Version), the
Revised Standard Version, and the New International
Version. Each of these has its strengths and weaknesses,
and none is beyond the possibility of improvement. Yet
each is a highly accurate translation, and someone reading
from any of them can be assured that he or she is reading
the Word of God in English.

The King James Version of the Bible is the most widely
circulated piece of literature ever produced. It was translated in 1611 and reflects the literary form of the period.
Major revisions of it were executed in 1629, 1638, 1762, and
1769. The most serious criticism of the King James Version
is that it was produced from what we now know to be an
inferior textual base for both Old and New Testaments.
The Greek text of the New Testament, for example, was
Erasmus's third edition and is based on a limited number
of late copies, which contained numerous errors and inter-
polations of copyists. Erasmus's text of Revelation lacked
the last six verses, and he supplied them by providing a
Greek retranslation from the Latin. A recent revision of the
King James Version was completed in 1982 and is published as the New King James Version. It has done an
admirable job of updating many archaic terms, which
mystify readers of the traditional King James text.

The Revised Standard Version, completed in 1952, represents an attempt to move from "formal equivalence" as a
translation principle to "dynamic equivalence." Formal
equivalence attempts to represent each word or phrase in
the donor text with a word or phrase in the receptor language; dynamic equivalence strives instead for a thought-
for-thought transfer from language to language and pays
particular attention to literary devices. The Hebrew and
Greek texts upon which this translation are based represent a considerable advance from those used for the King
James Version.

The New Testament section of the New International
Version was completed in 1973 and the Old Testament in
1978. It follows the dynamic-equivalence principle for

translation and is widely regarded as the most readable English version available to students of the sacred text. Its contemporary prose is nevertheless reverent and avoids slang or idiosyncratic language. Its translators were able to make use of the most current original-language sources, including the Dead Sea Scrolls.

The past few years have witnessed the publication and distribution of several "translations" (or, more correctly, "paraphrases") of the Word of God that are of limited usefulness. Usually called "modern-speech translations," these have been produced not by scholarly committees but by individuals who have occasionally read their theological presuppositions into their productions.

The New Testament in Modern English by J. B. Phillips, *Good News for Modern Man* by Robert Bratcher, and *The Living Bible Paraphrased* by Kenneth Taylor are examples of some of the most widely known works of this type. Each has its failures and objectionable treatments of certain biblical texts; each also has certain exceptionally well-done renderings. Whenever used, these should not be considered as standing on the level of the standard translations and should not be regarded as primary study texts. They should be viewed as *commentaries* on the text rather than translations of it, and therefore used with a reasonable degree of caution.

Conclusion

We can be confident about having God's Word in our possession. The Bibles we read today are not uncertain attempts to reproduce a distant and inadequately authenticated text.

After revealing, confirming, and recording the saving truth that constitutes the Bible, God has seen to its preservation and dissemination through the ages. That process of preservation has been almost as great a miracle as the original production of Scripture. It is probably impossible for us to be as grateful as we should be for having it in our possession.

8

"To Err Is Human"

In defense of the fallibility of our race, we say, "To err is human." Indeed! And to *fail* to err would be divine. Thus is summarized the final argument—a sort of negative argument—for the divine inspiration of the Bible. If the Bible is an integrated whole that contains no contradictions, errors of fact, or inconsistencies among its various human writers, it must be from God.

Someone may be ready to say, "But I've heard that the Bible does contain errors. In fact, I've heard that it is filled with mistakes." These alleged errors of Scripture are a slippery lot. The list keeps changing rapidly. In 1800, for example, the French Institute in Paris published a list of eighty-two errors in the Bible that they believed would destroy Christianity. Today not one of those "errors" remains to be resolved. Episodes of the sort described in chapter 5 of this volume have swept them away.

Research by historians, archaeologists, and scholars in a variety of fields has always settled disputes of fact in the biblical text in its favor. It gives believers considerable satisfaction to point out that not a single case of dispute over its credibility has ever been settled to the discredit of the Bible. Every battle over an alleged error in its pages that has been settled definitively has vindicated the Bible against its critics.

Christians regard truth as an integrated whole. All truth both derives from God and points back to him. Historical inaccuracies, internal contradiction, or factual errors of any sort would leave us without confidence in the book and the system of thought and life it offers. If the doctrine of biblical inerrancy is abandoned, the consequences would be disastrous for the Christian faith. There would be no way to be confident of knowing the will of God about anything. Even one's view of Jesus Christ would have to be altered radically, for Jesus unquestionably believed Scripture to be inerrant. Could he be the Son of God and teach a mistaken view of Scripture? Could a fallible person who dispensed false information be taken seriously as "God among us"? Could a fallible document that dispenses false information be taken seriously as the revelation to us of God's mind?

One who rejects the inerrancy of the Bible is simultaneously rejecting its authority as well. The Bible can be authoritative if, and only if, it is truly and verifiably the Word of God. That his word has been passed through men does not negate its authority so long as he has so controlled them as to guard them from all error. If his control over the biblical writers was not total, we can never be sure where the writer was accurate (thus believable) and where he was mistaken (thus worthy of rejection). In such a case, the Bible would be authoritative only when we declared it to be so. Then the circle has come full, and man is authoritative over the Bible rather than submitted to its direction.

That this is no misrepresentation of what is at stake can be seen from the following quotation from a writer who attempts to stand in the Christian tradition with regard to certain parts of Scripture while rejecting the doctrine of inerrancy: "I believe that the Bible is or ought to be authoritative for every Christian in all that it says on any subject unless and until he encounters a passage which after careful study and for good reason he cannot accept."[1]

The Bible is not a series of disjointed principles and occasional claims on the lives of men and women—and all this in a context of garbled factual reliability. Rather, it is a unified body of doctrine and commands that must stand or fall as a totality. Either all Scripture (every single passage) is from God and partakes of his perfection, or all Scripture should be set aside from its claimed and traditional role in the Christian religion.

Some Clarifications

The claim of this chapter—that the Bible is inerrant (infallible, without error)—and the use of that claim as a proof of its divine origin serves to complete the case for inspiration, which was begun in chapter 5. There are four clarifications that need to be made explicit and clear from the start.

1. *Inerrancy is claimed only for the original manuscripts of all the biblical books and not for later copies or translations of them.*

Different copyists over the years committed such slips as transposing words, altering the spelling of words, omitting or adding words, and occasionally even tampering with the text (cf. 1 John 5:7 in the King James Version). Having admitted that errors are contained in given copies of biblical materials, does this mean that we cannot be sure that the Bible we have is a faithful record of what was originally given? Absolutely not!

Perhaps the chief assurance that we know what was in the autographs lies in what one writer calls the "many-stranded cord of transmission." We have so many manuscripts of such nearness to the original documents that no knowledgeable student doubts the integrity of the text now available to us. As a summary of the previous chapter on text, transmission, and translation of the Bible, one should remember that " . . . the wealth of manuscripts, and above all the narrow interval of time between the writing and the earliest extant copies, make [the New Testament] by far the best attested text of any ancient writing in the world."[2] There is no question of consequence about one part in a thousand of our original-language biblical texts, and none of those remaining questions affects a single doctrine that is central to the Christian faith.

What, then, is the point of this clarification? It is to say that some alleged errors in Scripture are produced by people who cite a poor or faulty translation of the Bible. The answer to these problems will consist of an appeal to the underlying Hebrew or Greek text, for there is certainly no such thing as an infallible English translation of the Bible.

2. *Inerrancy does not imply verbal exactness of quotations.*

The words Jesus spoke while on the cross may not be given with word-for-word correspondence by the Synoptic writers. Quotations from the Old Testament may not correspond exactly with either the Massoretic Text or the Septuagint. In cases such as these, the writer may be giving the sense of the quotation rather than attempting an exact quote. Most of us do the same thing commonly and without rebuke.

If a critic is not careful, he may find himself imposing artificial standards of accuracy on Scripture that he does not observe in any other context. For example, suppose he told three of his friends, "My daughter is hospitalized with pneumonia." Friend One went home and told his wife, "Critic told me his little girl is sick." Friend Two bumped into a mutual friend and told him, "Say, have you heard that Critic's daughter is in the hospital?" Friend Three, arriving at the place where he and Critic both work, went to the boss and said, "Boss, you should know that Critic will be late for work today—if he gets here at all—because his child is very sick."

In the scenario above, which of the three friends got it right? They all did. Though not one of them quoted Critic with a word-for-word exactness, each one gave the true sense of what he knew. The writers of the Synoptics or other biblical materials are entitled to the same right.

3. *Inerrancy does not require verbal agreement in parallel accounts of the same event.*

The Spirit-guided writers addressed different readers for different purposes, so their accounts of the same event may have been given in different words. But there are no contradictions. In fact, by putting the different accounts together, one often comes up with a more complete picture of the episode than any one account could provide.

Take the Synoptic Gospels (Matthew, Mark, and Luke) as a case in point. Matthew was written by a Jewish apostle who told of events he witnessed in a document written to other Jews who knew the Old Testament as he did. But Mark was written for Gentile readers by a Jewish disciple who had received the bulk of his information about Jesus from Peter rather than through firsthand experience with the Nazarene. Finally comes Luke, the only Gospel written by a Greek for other Greeks, whose writer's knowledge of Jesus came through the study of documents others had written about him and oral reports he had heard. From their different backgrounds and sources, the Synoptists wrote to different audiences about Jesus of Nazareth.

By way of analogy, three witnesses to an event who testified about it in court would hardly be expected to give their testimony with precise verbal agreement. In fact, doing so would compromise their integrity because it would suggest collusion and possibly fraudulent testimony. We would expect each witness to give an account of what he knew in his own words and from his own unique perspective. It is therefore strange to have these same factors of personality and perspective discounted with the biblical writers.

4. *The Bible uses popular expressions rather than technical language to express ideas.*

Scripture does not err when it speaks of the "four corners of the earth" or the "rising of the sun." It is simply using common speech forms which are still common in our scientific time. Figures of speech and idioms are used freely in the books of the Bible and enhance its appeal as literature.

Any document under investigation must be studied by an appropriate and sound hermeneutic. Hebrew poetry, for example, is quite different in structure and nature from what we call poetry in modern English-speaking countries. It would be irresponsible to use the standards of English poetry to judge biblical or nonbiblical Hebrew literature in poetic form. Then there is a special class of Hebrew literature known as "apocalyptic," which has peculiar features all its own. The Old Testament's Book of Ezekiel and the New Testament's Book of Revelation are good examples of apocalyptic writing. Failure to interpret them according to their correct genre has resulted in fantastic interpretations and claimed contradictions between these and other canonical documents.

What Shall We Define as "Error"?

As we prepare to look at some alleged errors in Scripture, we must be sure to define what will count as a genuine "error" in the Bible. In view of the fact that the Bible has been vindicated so many times against the charge of containing errors, one could become suspicious that there is a spirit of negative criticism among some that causes them to place every difficulty in the scriptural text on their list of errors. Is that a legitimate approach?

In the study of ancient documents such as Plato's dialogues, classicists, historians, and philosophers generally observe what is called "the principle of charity." If statements within a given dialogue seem to differ from those found in another, respect for the genius of Plato causes the scholars studying them to look first for a possible harmonization. If there emerges a plausible harmony that is consistent with the total Platonic corpus, the charge of error, inconsistency, or contradiction is considered unjustified. Only in the absence of a reasonable solution does one charge Plato with contradicting himself.

Believers ask nothing more for the Bible. Where a reasonable solution of a biblical difficulty can be offered, there is no justification for maintaining the presence of error or contradiction. As an international panel of thirty-four scholars concluded in a 1987 study titled *The Historical Reliability of the Gospels*: "It is fair to say that all the alleged inconsistencies among the Gospels have received at least plausible solutions." Some of the evidence appropriate to their conclusion will be presented in this chapter.

Even Peter admitted that Paul's epistles "contain some things that are hard to understand" (2 Peter 3:16). Therefore, one should not be surprised to find some statements and issues in Scripture that puzzle good and honest minds. The Bible's negative critics must not claim for themselves the infallibility they are denying to Scripture in order to criticize it. It is always possible that what looks like an inconsistency or mistake is due to the critic's own lack of knowledge of the language, culture, history, or some other feature of the document in question.

Moving now to specifics, attention will focus on a series of alleged errors in the Gospels. Since previous chapters have looked at several Old Testament texts and Acts, the spotlight here will be on the first four books of the New Testament.

Some Alleged Errors in the Gospels

The texts chosen for examination below have been selected for two reasons. First, they are among those commonly cited by negative critics when asked to produce examples of biblical errors. Second, they all center on the life and person of Christ and will provide background to the next section of this book, which will deal with the issue of his deity.

Setting for Jesus' Birth

One of the places in the Gospels where critics have alleged to find historical errors is in the setting given for the birth of Jesus in Luke's Gospel: "In those days Caesar Augustus issued a decree that a census should be taken of the entire Roman world. (This was the first census that took place while Quirinius was governor of Syria.) And everyone went to his own town to register" (Luke 2:1–3).

It has been asserted that this opening statement to the birth narrative is hopelessly confused on three counts: (1) there was no general census taken under Augustus; (2) Quirinius was not governing Syria at the time in question; and (3) a Roman census did not require travel to one's ancestral home but registered people at their place of residence.

First, we now know from archaeological finds that enrollments did occur under Roman auspices every fourteen years. Luke calls this one "the first census" to distinguish it from one taken in A.D. 6, which he later mentioned at Acts 5:37 and which is also cited by Josephus.[3] Archaeologists have found actual census documents from A.D. 34 and other undated census documents that are believed to be from A.D. 20 or possibly even the census of A.D. 6. Counting back fourteen years from A.D. 6, one arrives at 8 B.C. as the date for the census of Luke 2. This fixes a census under Augustus at the approximate time of the birth of Jesus.

Second, it is true that in the nonbiblical documents of the period, Quirinius is said to have become governor of Syria in A.D. 6 and Saturninus was governor during the period corresponding to Christ's birth. Again, archaeologists have now found data confirming the biblical record. An inscription found at Tiber and later substantiated by another from Antioch establishes that Quirinius twice governed Syria as imperial legate. The first time was between 10 and 7 B.C. Thus, when Saturninus was procurator of Syria, Quirinius was the military governor.[4]

Third, the unlikely business of requiring people to return to their family homes for registration did occur in some Roman enrollments. A rescript from neighboring Egypt dated A.D. 104 says: "The enrollment by household being at hand, it is necessary to notify all who for any cause soever are outside their own administrative district that they return at once to their homes in order to carry out the customary procedure of enrollment. . . ."[5]

As Sir William Ramsay learned from his experiences with Acts, Luke is a very careful historian and has given details of the census that only someone who lived close to it and looked into the event closely would have been able to provide.[6]

Two Genealogies for Jesus

It is sometimes alleged that the Gospels contradict one another in the lineage they trace for Jesus of Nazareth. The genealogy found at Matthew 1:1–16 is remarkably different from the one found at Luke 3:23–38.

As was noted above, Matthew and Luke wrote from very different backgrounds and for very different audiences. They therefore offered different—but not contradictory—genealogies of Jesus. Matthew wrote to Jews and offered his legal lineage through Joseph; Luke wrote to Gentiles and gave his actual descent through Mary.

Under Jewish law and tradition, any claim of Davidic descent and title to the Davidic throne would have to be established through the father's side of the family. Although the New Testament insists that Joseph was not the actual father of Jesus, the fact remains that he was his legal father-guardian. So Matthew gave Jesus' lineage through Joseph and established the clear relationship to David, which would be necessary for him to assert a claim to being the Messiah.

On the other hand, Luke wrote for Greek readers who would have had no concern for the demands of Jewish law. From reading Luke 1 and 2, it seems that the story of the birth of Jesus is told from Mary's perspective. In fact, he begins the genealogy by saying that Jesus was not really Joseph's son at all—though an uninformed public generally supposed he was (cf. Luke 3:23). If he was not Joseph's son, why should Joseph's lineage be given to Luke's readers? Thus, he gave the actual bloodline through Mary, starting with Joseph's father-in-law (Heli) and tracing all the way back to Adam.

Far from contradictory, the two genealogies serve the very useful purpose of establishing the full family tree of the Son of man.

"Uzziah the Father of Jotham"

Before leaving the genealogies of Jesus, another problem associated with the one in Matthew can be addressed. Matthew 1:9 speaks of "Uzziah the father of Jotham." Yet 2 Kings 15:1–7 and 1 Chronicles 3:12 give the father of Jotham as Azariah.

"The father of Jotham" is one of many Bible characters who bears more than one name. The list includes Abraham (Abram), Sarah (Sarai), Jacob (Israel), Gideon (Jerubbaal), Jehoiakim (Eliakim), Jehoiachin (Jeconiah, Coniah), Paul (Saul), and many others.

The textual proof of this is found in 2 Kings 15. Although verses 1–7 call Jotham's father Azariah, verses 32 and 34 use his alternative name, Uzziah. Unless we feel forced to conclude that the writer was such a fool that he could not remember a man's name from one line on the page to another shortly after it, we can reasonably say that the writer was citing alternative names for the sake of later readers who might know Jotham's father by one designation rather than the other.

Matthew's Quotation of Micah 5:2

Some critics indict Matthew for misquoting the Old Testament in the birth narratives of Jesus and charge that he tampered significantly with the meaning of the text in question. In fact, Matthew does appear to conflate Micah 5:2 and 2 Samuel 5:2 in citing an Old Testament prophecy about the birth of the Messiah. From the Essene commentaries on the Bible found in the Dead Sea Scrolls, we know that this sort of blending of texts was common at the time. While admitting that the quotation is not word-for-word with either the Massoretic Text of the Hebrew Bible or the Septuagint's rendering of the verse into Greek, there is nothing inaccurate about Matthew's citation. He gives the true sense of the verse(s) in question and applies them to Jesus with a consummate literary artistry. And, as was observed earlier in this chapter, the giving of a text's true sense rather than a verbally exact citation is the commonest way all of us cite biblical or other texts.

"Though you are small among the clans of Judah" (Mic. 5:2) becomes "[You] are by no means least among the rulers of Judah" (Matt. 2:6). First, Bethlehem was indeed a "small" town in both Old and New Testament times; that fact was generally known. Yet, because the Messiah was born there, Bethlehem certainly would be "by no means least" (in terms of significance) among the cities of antiquity.

The difference between "clans of Judah" and "rulers of Judah" is hardly problematic at all. Matthew may well preserve an alternative reading of the Hebrew text by reading *'alluphe* (rulers) for *'alphe* (thousands). This would involve no change in the consonantal spelling of the word in question, and the vowel points customarily used by today's Old Testament scholars and translators were not supplied until about the eighth century A.D.

The Order of the Temptations

Is there a contradiction between Matthew and Luke on the order of Jesus' wilderness temptations? (cf. Matt. 4:1–11; Luke 4:1–13).

There is certainly a difference in the order. Matthew and Luke both place first the temptation to turn stones to bread. Matthew next tells of the temptation to leap from the temple wall and then of the temptation to bow down and worship Satan. Luke reverses the order of these two.

In the first place, neither writer asserts that he is following a strict chronological sequence in relating the encounter. Matthew's order appears to be more logical than chronological—moving from physical hunger through personal pride to the question of ultimate allegiance. Luke's order, on the other hand, seems more natural to the geographical sequence one might expect—with the first two temptations in the wilderness and the third in the city of Jerusalem.

In the second place, a demand is being made of these two writers that we do not ordinarily make of other reporters. Suppose my daughter tells me about her day and says, "It was awful. I missed lunch, had to take two exams at school, and was late getting to work. On top of it all, I had an accident in my car." All the facts are present, but they may be in something other than chronological order. Is her report therefore incorrect? Was her day other than she described? The precise order may have been exams, accident, missed lunch, and late arrival for work. The difference in order is hardly the issue, however, in either the temptation accounts in the Gospels or in the report of my daughter's eventful day.

Matthew 16:28 as a Failed Prophecy

Against the many predictions and fulfillments that believers point to as proof that the Bible is inspired, skeptics and unbelievers seek evidence for failed or unfulfilled prophecies in Scripture. One frequently alleged failure is Jesus' prediction: "I tell you the truth, some who are standing here will not taste death before they see the Son of Man coming in his kingdom" (Matt. 16:28). We are reminded that the end of the world has not come yet—much less did it occur in the lifetime of Jesus' contemporaries.

The kingdom of God will reach its ultimate and climactic phase at the visible return of Christ at the end of the age. Preliminary phases of that kingdom are also referred to in Scripture, and this fact provides the key to understanding this predictive prophecy. The allegation of a failed prophecy is founded on a misinterpretation of what the text actually predicts.

Staying within the Gospel of Matthew, we note that Jesus had previously said:

> I tell you the truth: Among those born of women there has
> not risen anyone greater than John the Baptist; yet he who
> is least in the kingdom of heaven is greater than he. From
> the days of John the Baptist until now, the kingdom of
> heaven has been forcefully advancing, and forceful men lay
> hold of it (Matt. 11:11–12).

In a preliminary phase, the kingdom was among men in
the Baptist's time; at a fuller phase of its arrival, those
entering it would be superior to John. That time came on
the first Pentecost following the resurrection of Jesus,
when the Holy Spirit came upon the apostles and the
church was founded (Acts 2). That event took place in the
lifetime of many who were present to hear Jesus make the
statement of Matthew 16:28.

Furthermore, when John the gospel writer recorded
Jesus' final night with the apostles, he told of a promise
made then. Having plunged the apostles into despair by
telling them he was going away (John 14:1–4), Jesus
pledged, "I will not leave you as orphans; I will come to
you" (John 14:18). He added that both he and the Father
would come and make their home with them (John 14:23).
How would he leave them, yet come again to them? He
would come in the person and activity of the Holy Spirit.

> But the Counselor, the Holy Spirit, whom the Father will
> send in my name, will teach you all things and will remind
> you of everything I have said. . . . You heard me say, "I
> am going away and I am coming back to you." . . . I have
> told you now before it happens, so that when it does hap-
> pen you will believe (John 14:26–29).

The Spirit came in fulfillment of this prediction on the
Pentecost Day recorded in Acts 2. Far from being an example of a failed prophecy, this is a case of one that has been
fulfilled at a specific time and place we can identify with
certainty. The fulfillment of this prophecy as specified (in
the lifetime of Jesus' contemporaries) assures us that the

final phase of the kingdom will one day be realized at his personal second coming.

Sending Out the Twelve

The Synoptics tell how Jesus sent out the apostles on a preaching tour during his public ministry. His instructions are recorded in Matthew 10:5–16, Mark 6:8–11, and Luke 9:3–5. According to the negative critics' analysis of these accounts, the writers contradict each other in the details of what the apostles were allowed to carry on their tour. Mark permits them to wear sandals and carry a staff; Matthew has them required to go barefoot; Luke forbids the staff but says nothing about sandals one way or another.

At first blush, these three texts seem to present a considerable problem. Upon close inspection, however, what seems to be a significant problem turns out to be manageable in its proportions.

Initially one should see the general setting of this episode. The apostles were being sent out to preach the gospel of the kingdom and were asked to trust God to supply their needs. Instead of rounding up support for their mission, they were to go, trusting God to provide for them.

Against this general background, the specific requirements were to the effect that they not take "extra" tunics, sandals, or staffs. This assumes that most (if not all) of the group were clothed with a tunic, were wearing sandals, and likely had staffs. They could take what they had but were not to take the time to secure extra items to supplement their meager fare. If we understand the prohibition against staff and sandals to be absolute rather than relative (none at all rather than none beyond their daily custom), a contradiction does exist among the passages. But if relative rather than absolute, there is none.

At least two compelling lines of evidence support the latter understanding.

First, the Greek word used by Matthew and translated "take" (Matt. 10:9) is *ktesesthe* and means "procure for oneself, acquire, get."[7] Matthew thus supplements our under-standing of Jesus' precise requirement. They were not to take the time to *acquire* a staff if they did not already have one; but Mark 6:8 seems to imply that this did not require discarding one already in hand.

Second, the Talmud prohibits worshipers from going onto the temple grounds with staff, shoes, scrip, or money tied to their persons. They were to enter that sacred area with only such things as could be carried in hand.[8] Jesus apparently chose to send out his messengers in the same spirit by forbidding them to bother with the extra provisions that travelers of the time generally considered neces-sary. At the same time, however, he did not send them out deprived of the bare essentials with which they would nor-mally leave home in the morning.

Healing Blindness at Jericho

The Synoptics tell of the healing of blindness at Jericho toward the end of Jesus' public career (Matt. 20:29–34; Mark 10:46–52; Luke 18:35–43). Detractors are quick to point out things in these accounts that they regard as seri-ous inconsistencies, if not outright errors. Matthew and Mark say the event took place as Jesus left Jericho, whereas Luke appears to say it happened as he approached the city. Matthew reports two blind men to have been involved, whereas Mark and Luke mention only one. Mark gives the name "Bartimaeus" in his account, but the other writers give no names.

The second and third issues seem to be so trivial as to merit little attention. If two men were healed, it would not be unthinkable that one of the two was more impressive or colorful than the other. Thus, a writer might tell the story in terms of him, one even citing his name. There would be a contradiction only if Mark or Luke had said there was only one blind man involved.

The real challenge here has to do with whether Jesus was entering or leaving Jericho when the event happened. He could not have been doing both. Or could he? A possible solution to this difficult text comes from archaeology. The Old Testament city of Canaanite Jericho was near the New Testament city of the same name. It is possible that Jesus healed the blind men after walking through the old city and as he entered the new.

Another possibility sees the story as a long and complicated affair, which is told only briefly by each writer. Our confusion arises from the fact that we have only snatches rather than a step-by-step narrative of the day's events.

Looking closely at Luke's account, for example, it is clear that three major events took place on that day in Jericho: the healing of the blind beggar (18:35–43), the encounter with Zacchaeus (19:1–10), and the teaching of the Parable of the Ten Minas (19:11–27). Although the stories are isolated from each other for the purpose of telling them, it is fully conceivable that the encounter with the blind man ran through a long period of time—starting with his first cry for Jesus' help as the rabbi from Nazareth entered Jericho and ending with his healing as he left it.

Reading the text closely, we see Luke telling that the blind man was begging beside the road as Jesus entered Jericho. The commotion of Jesus' arrival caused the beggar to ask who the celebrity was. When he found out that it was Jesus, he had apparently heard enough about this man from Nazareth to believe that he could be healed by him. Thus he cried, "Jesus, Son of David, have mercy on me!" In the noise of the crowd, perhaps he was not even heard at that point. It is unknown to us how long he followed the crowd, faltering because of his handicap, before he could be heard by Jesus. The second blind man may have joined him somewhere along the route. Assuming that the excitement of the crowd would have abated as the day wore on, it could well be argued as more likely that the blind man would receive Jesus' attention with his cries as the teacher was leaving rather than at the time of his entry. Then he was healed.

These two possible solutions are conjectural. There is simply not enough information to allow us to claim that all the difficulties here are resolved beyond question. At the same time, however, the difficulties are not without the possibility of a plausible solution. It would therefore be presumptuous for a critic to use this as a case of proved error in the Bible.

Who Carried the Cross?

It is sometimes asserted that there is an inconsistency in the Gospels with regard to carrying the cross of Jesus. John 19:17 has Jesus leaving Pilate's judgment hall "carrying his own cross," whereas the Synoptics say it was carried by a certain Simon of Cyrene (cf. Matt. 27:32; Mark 15:21; Luke 23:26). Which was it?

Given that Jesus had apparently not slept all night and had been flogged to within an inch of his life, it is reasonable to put the accounts together and see him leaving Pilate carrying his own cross, becoming too weak to carry it very far, and Simon being forced by a soldier to step up and draw the crossbeam the remainder of the way to Golgotha.

Such an interpretation is neither forced nor fanciful. Rather, it corresponds with the detail given in Mark that Simon "was passing by on his way in from the country, and they forced him to carry the cross." Simon would not have been "passing by" Pilate's judgment hall on his way in from the country. But such language is perfectly appropriate to someone who was working his way into town against the movement of a crowd headed toward the crucifixion site.

The Time of the Crucifixion

A long-standing criticism of the consistency of the Gospel records focuses on Mark's statement that Jesus was crucified at "the third hour" of the day (Mark 15:25) set over against John's that his trial before Pilate was still in progress at "about the sixth hour" (John 19:14). How can these accounts be harmonized?

For one thing, our penchant for precise times can hardly

be accommodated by documents from antiquity. Without clocks or even calendars of the sort we use, rough approximations are the best we get in ancient literature.

Furthermore, there were at least two major ways of counting time in use during Jesus' time. One way counted from sundown to sunrise to sundown—marking time in twelve-hour increments from either dusk (the third hour of evening) or dawn (the third hour of day). The other counted from midnight to noon to midnight—marking time in twelve-hour increments from either. There is always a question of which method is being used by a writer, either in the Gospels or in other literature of the period.

Since it is most unlikely that Mark has Jesus being crucified at 3:00 A.M. (counting from midnight), it seems safe to assume that he places the event at roughly 9:00 A.M. (counting "the third hour" from sunrise). If, on the other hand, John was counting from midnight (counting "the sixth hour" from midnight, or around 6:00 A.M.), the problem vanishes. If the trial started at dawn—and the events of betrayal night seem to have been continual through the hours of darkness—the trip to Golgotha and other preliminaries of the morning would have placed the hour of crucifixion at around 9:00 A.M.

Based on John 1:39, there is good reason to think John used the Roman method of counting from midnight. When two disciples went off with Jesus and "spent that day with him," it is hardly possible that the counting begins with sunrise. If so, the "day" would be only from about 4:00 P.M. until 6:00 P.M. If, on the other hand, the counting is understood from midnight, the full day's events can be fitted easily into a 10:00 A.M.-until-evening period.

How Did Judas Die?

Negative critics of the Bible frequently question the details of Judas's death. Matthew 27:5 says he hanged himself, but Acts 1:18–19 records Peter's statement to the effect that he "fell headlong" into a field and burst open.

A tragic account of suicide carried in newspapers across

the United States a few years ago told of a man who shot himself in the head while sitting on an upper-level ledge of a multi-story building. The story might have been told in at least three different ways: (1) he shot himself in the head with a pistol; (2) he fell several stories to the sidewalk below; or (3) he fell to the sidewalk after shooting himself on the building's ledge. Which would be the correct way to tell it? All three would be correct.

The apparent sequence of events in Judas's death involved remorse and depression, return of the thirty pieces of silver to the priests with whom he had bargained, hanging himself, his body's decomposing for a time, and eventually his body's falling from the hanging site and bursting open. That "his body burst open and all his intestines spilled out" (Acts 1:18) is unlikely from the most severe of falls unless some degree of decomposition and distension had already occurred.

Since money wrongly acquired could not be put into the temple treasury (cf. Deut. 23:18), the priests apparently used the thirty pieces of silver to purchase a potter's field. Ironically, it was in that very field that Judas fell after his suicide by hanging. It is a tragic tale, but there is no contradiction in the biblical accounts of it.

Conclusion

In the spring of 1983, the attention of the world was focused on what would have been the publishing phenomenon of the post-World War II Western world. Gerd Heidemann, a reporter for the German magazine *Stern*, claimed to have uncovered sixty volumes of secret diaries of Adolf Hitler and two more volumes of other writings from the man who triggered that awful war. At the end of what Heidemann claimed was a three- to four-year search through Germany, Spain, and South America, the diaries were supposedly going to shed new light on the Third Reich.

At a press conference in Hamburg, *Stern* editor Peter

Koch said, "I am 100 percent convinced that Hitler wrote every single word in those books." The London *Sunday Times* purchased publication rights to the diaries, said they had been authenticated by historians and handwriting experts, and started printing the materials. *Newsweek* carried a cover story on the diaries. Within a matter of days, they had been exposed as forgeries. There were anachronisms, repeated historical slips, and inconsistencies in the manuscripts. *Stern* filed fraud charges against Heidemann, and there was major embarrassment among the "experts" who had gone on record in favor of the authenticity of the diaries.

The swift and fatal discrediting of the alleged Hitler diaries stands in positive contrast to the way the Bible has survived the closest possible scrutiny over the centuries. It has been—and continues to be—criticized by unbelievers. But when the evidence comes in, Scripture stands vindicated. Again. And again. And again.

Yes, there are difficult texts. And there are passages where the necessary evidence that would decide the issue once and for all is not available because of the antiquity of certain events. But, after centuries of studying its books, pages, and words, there are no signs of forgery. The book is undeniably the *Word of God*.

9

God with a Human Face

According to a commonly circulated account of their meeting, when Napoleon met the German scholar Wieland in 1808, he asked not about political or military matters but whether he believed in the historical reality of Jesus of Nazareth. "The Jesus Question" haunts every heart, for no one can escape the necessity of reacting to him in some way. To worship him, if he is *not* divine, is nothing less than idolatry; to fail to worship him, if he *is* divine, is sacrilege of the highest order.

The claims of the New Testament evangelists about Jesus are both extraordinary and unequaled.

> You are the Christ, the Son of the living God (Peter in Matt. 16:16).

> Salvation is found in no one else, for there is no other name under heaven given to men by which we must be saved (Peter in Acts 4:12).

> Therefore God exalted him to the highest place
> and gave him the name that is above every name,
> that at the name of Jesus every knee should bow,
> in heaven and on earth and under the earth,
> and every tongue confess that Jesus Christ is Lord,
> to the glory of God the Father (Paul in Phil. 2:9–11).

For there is one God and one mediator between God and
men, the man Christ Jesus, who gave himself a ransom for
all men (Paul in 1 Tim. 2:5–6a).

It is not that these claims about Jesus were made by
fanatically devoted disciples against his will. The claims
made by them were the outgrowth of the claims he had
previously made for himself. He identified himself with
Yahweh of the Old Testament patriarchs (John 8:31–59). He
claimed the authority to forgive sins, an authority that God
alone could have (Mark 2:5-7). He dared to say, "I and the
Father are one" and was immediately accused of blasphe-
my by his critics because such a statement emphatically
asserted his deity (John 10:30-33). He claimed to have an
unparalleled and unshared sonship to God the Father
(Matt. 11:27).

When Jesus of Nazareth stood face to face with the high
priest of the Jewish nation, Caiaphas said, "I charge you
under oath by the living God: Tell us if you are the Christ,
the Son of God." To this direct challenge, Jesus replied,
"Yes, it is as you say" (Matt. 26:63–64).

Claims of such magnitude cannot be ignored. They are
either true or false. They must be believed or rejected. If
they are accepted as true and believed, profound implications follow for every aspect of one's life. If they are
thrown out as false and repudiated, one stands either to
deny the existence of God altogether or else to propose
another means of access into his favor. Any attempt to be
neutral to Jesus of Nazareth is tantamount to rejecting him.

In the next three chapters a case will be made for the historicity, deity, humanity, and redemptive role of Jesus
Christ. Recalling the question of the Russian writer who
affirmed his faith in a "supreme reason" in the universe
but wondered if that being knew (or cared) about him,
these chapters will answer in the affirmative. They will
build on the facts already in evidence about God's existence and the inspiration of the Bible to prove that Jesus is

who he claimed to be and that his bold and exclusive claims to be the Savior of the world are true.

The goal of Christian apologetics is not merely to prove that the fundamental doctrines of the faith are true, but to ask people who have been convinced of their truthfulness to allow Jesus Christ to save them. Thus, apologetics is a means to the larger task of evangelism. The message of devoted Christians from the first century to the present has remained the same: "For we do not preach ourselves, but Jesus Christ as Lord, and ourselves as your servants for Jesus' sake" (2 Cor. 4:5).

In this chapter, we will examine our sources of information about Jesus—both nonbiblical and biblical—and what they reveal about his impact on history and his personal character. Chapter 10 will focus on the critical issues of predictive prophecy and miraculous signs, which prove that he is the Son of God and Savior of the world. Special attention will be focused on the event of his resurrection from the dead. Then chapter 11 will examine the specific content of his bold and exclusive claim to be the *only* Redeemer. The claim that the Christian religion is the one true religion that leads to salvation and eternal life will be made, explained, and defended.

The Historicity of Jesus

Unlike the Greek mythologies or the irrational tales of Eastern religions, the religion of Jesus Christ alleges that its central events occurred in the arena of history and are subject to the same sort of investigation that all other historical events invite. In making his case for the resurrection, for example, Paul wrote of the various people who had seen Jesus alive after his crucifixion under Pontius Pilate. Among those eyewitnesses, he claimed, Jesus "appeared to more than five hundred of the brothers at the same time, most of whom are still living . . . " (1 Cor. 15:6). There is no mistaking Paul's point in this statement. If someone wants to know what happened, he can interview the witnesses.

Paul could invite his contemporaries to interview persons associated with Jesus and the resurrection event. Although we live nearly twenty centuries too late to accept the challenge Paul gave in the mid-first century, we are not too late to make our own meaningful investigations about Jesus. After all, neither do we have firsthand knowledge of Alexander the Great; nor can we interview the personal acquaintances of George Washington to learn about his presidency. We do have generally accepted and well-tested means of making inquiries about both these figures, however, and we speak of them and events from their lives without apprehension. The same methods of historical investigation may be—and ought to be—applied to Jesus of Nazareth.

Challenges to the historicity of Jesus are very rare today, though occasionally someone will advance the thesis that there was no historical Jesus of Nazareth and that "he is an idea gradually constructed and modified over a considerable period of time."[1] People who have never studied the many proofs of his historical authenticity are usually astounded by the wealth of evidence about him when it is brought to their attention.

Although our primary documents for information about Jesus are the four Gospels, we could construct a rather complete outline of his career from Roman and Jewish historians.

Roman Sources

The Roman historian Tacitus wrote of Nero and the terrible fire at Rome in July of A.D. 64. He tells how some of the citizens suspected the emperor himself of having put the city to the torch and of Nero's wicked attempt to divert suspicion from himself.

> Consequently, to get rid of the report, Nero fastened the guilt and inflicted the most exquisite tortures on a class hated for their abominations, called Christians by the populace. Christus, from whom the name had its origin, suf-

fered the extreme penalty during the reign of Tiberius at the hands of one of our procurators, Pontius Pilate, and a most mischievous superstition thus checked for the moment, again broke out not only in Judea, the first source of the evil, but even in Rome, where all things hideous and shameful from every part of the world find their center and become popular.[2]

As the tone of this report suggests, Tacitus was not a Christian or a friend of Christians. If anything, that makes his report more important from a historical perspective. This is not "propaganda" from people trying to invent a character. It is the matter-of-fact report by an unsympathetic historian about the presence and impact of a Jewish religious figure. It was written *ca.* A.D. 115.

At roughly the same time, another Roman historian recorded some information of interest. Suetonius, writing of the career of Claudius (emperor of Rome A.D. 41–54), says: "Since the Jews constantly made disturbances at the instigation of Chrestus, he expelled them from Rome."[3] The reference to "Chrestus" is probably an alternative spelling of "Christ," and the "disturbances" referred to are most likely the sort of conflicts that occurred frequently in the first-century world when Christians went to, taught in, and won converts from the Jewish synagogues. Although not a direct reference to the life of Jesus, this record from Suetonius proves the existence of the Christian movement in Rome within twenty years of the death of Jesus of Nazareth.

A contemporary of Tacitus and Suetonius was a man named Pliny. He was not an historian, but he has provided valuable information to historians through an extensive correspondence, which has been preserved. Around A.D. 111, Pliny was appointed to serve as imperial legate of the province of Bithynia in Asia Minor. While filling that post, he carried on an amazing exchange of letters with the emperor. He wrote long letters, which give the details of situations that were facing him, and asked help from his emperor in knowing what to do in response to them. Writing to Trajan (emperor, A.D. 98–117), he explained his problem in conducting trials of persons accused of being Christians.

> An anonymous document was laid before me containing many people's names. Some of these denied they were Christians or had ever been so; at my dictation they invoked the gods and did reverence with incense and wine to your image, which I had ordered to be brought for this purpose along with the statues of the gods; they also cursed Christ; and as I am informed that people who are really Christians cannot possibly be made to do any of those things, I considered that the people who did them should be discharged.[4]

The letter goes on to give more interesting details of Pliny's relations with Christians. In particular, it gives a moving account of the sort of worship the Christians conducted. For our purposes, however, it is sufficient to note that Jesus Christ is referred to without any thought of denying his historicity.

The late Will Durant, a respected historian who was an unbeliever with reference to the deity of Jesus, considered this question and wrote: "The denial of that existence seems never to have occurred even to the bitterest gentile or Jewish opponents of nascent Christianity."[5] This fact alone weighs heavily against any present-day skeptic who might feel inclined to challenge his existence. Of the alternative possibility that Jesus is a mythical creation of human imagination, Durant said: "That a few simple men should in one generation have invented so powerful and appealing a personality, so lofty an ethic and so inspiring a vision of human brotherhood, would be a miracle far more incredible than any recorded in the Gospels."[6]

Jewish Sources

Besides these Roman sources, there are also references to Jesus in several important Jewish sources.

Josephus was born in A.D. 37 or 38 to a priestly family of Judea and was educated in the rabbinic tradition. When the ill-fated revolt against Rome broke out in Palestine in A.D. 66, he joined the resistance fighters and was appointed commander of the Jewish forces in Galilee. Captured the next year and brought before General Vespasian, he predicted that the general would become the emperor of Rome. For reasons we do not understand, Vespasian spared his life and had Josephus held in prison. When Vespasian did become emperor in A.D. 69, he remembered Josephus, ordered him set free, and eventually rewarded him a pension.

Josephus devoted the remainder of his life to writing Jewish history under Roman patronage. Since much of what he wrote was contemporary with the composition of the New Testament, his works are sometimes quite valuable in giving us background information to many persons and events referred to in Scripture. For example, he mentions the death of John the Baptist in his narrative about Herod Antipas.[7] He also tells of the death of James, "the brother of Jesus, the so-called Christ."[8]

The most detailed reference to Jesus in his works is questionable as it stands. We have a total of three Greek manuscripts of Josephus's *Antiquities*, and none of them is older than the eleventh century. In those texts, Jesus is acknowledged as a miracle worker and called "the Messiah." His resurrection on the third day is also admitted. There are good reasons to think this paragraph has been tampered with by Christian copyists. Admitting that our received text of Josephus has been altered to include confessions he would not have made, the fact remains that modern scholarship is generally convinced that it builds upon an authentic reference to Jesus.

An article by Paul Winter distinguishes three types of statements in our received texts of this passage: (1) parts not compatible with a Christian interpolator's outlook; (2) parts not compatible with Josephus's known views; and (3) parts that are of such a neutral character that they could have been written either by the Jew Josephus or by a later Christian interpolator.[9] In the first category are several expressions that are altogether characteristic of Josephus but inadequate for any Christian who is seeking to give praise to his Lord.

In its original form, the paragraph in question likely would have read something like this:

> Now there arose about this time a source of further trouble in one Jesus, a wise man who performed surprising works, a teacher of men who gladly welcome strange things. He led away many Jews, and also many of the Gentiles. He was the so-called Christ. When Pilate, acting on information supplied by the chief men among us, condemned him to the cross, those who had attached themselves to him at first did not cease to cause trouble, and the tribe of Christians, which has taken this name from him, is not extinct even today.[10]

It is significant to note that two translations of the *Antiquities* survive to us from sources independent of our extant Greek copies. An Arabic version from the tenth century and an Old Russian version from the eleventh or twelfth century do not have the historical value of the three Greek copies already mentioned. Both of them do contain the disputed reference to Jesus, however, without the evidence of Christian tampering found in the Greek manuscripts.

The oral interpretations of the Law of Moses given by the leading rabbis of the first two centuries of the Christian era were codified as the Mishnah in the third century. Additional commentary on the Mishnah produced the Talmud in Jerusalem in the fourth century and in Babylon in the fifth. The references to Jesus in these documents are significant for the Jewish perspective they give on Jesus. Most references to Jesus are, of course, derogatory in nature. Thus, he is referred to as "a certain person" or "Balaam." In some Talmudic texts, Jesus is called "Ben

Stada" or "Ben Panthera." Since "ben" means "son of," the clear implication is to his illegitimacy.

Foremost among the rabbis who give information about Jesus is Rabbi Eliezer, whose teacher, Rabbi Johanan ben Zakkai, was a contemporary of Jesus.

> It is tradition that Rabbi Eliezer said to the wise, "Did not Ben Stada bring spells from Egypt in a cut which was upon his flesh?" They said to him, "He was a fool, and they do bring a proof from a fool." Rabbi Hisda said, "The husband was Stada, the paramour was Pandira." The husband was Pappos ben Jehudah, the father was Stada. The mother was Miriam the dresser of women's hair; as we say in Pembeditha, "Such a one has been false to her husband."[11]

With its vague reference to the cut in his flesh and the disparagement of both Jesus and his mother, texts such as this admit his existence. The attempt by the enemies of Christianity was to try to discredit him, but there was no effort to dismiss him as mythical. They presuppose his actual existence. Not one of them attempts to cast doubt on the fact that he was a real character of human history who lived at the time and under the circumstances described in the New Testament.

If we did not have a Bible, then, we would know the name and general life outline of the person Jesus of Nazareth. We would also know the gist of the claims he made for himself and something of the powerful impact he made on the world at the beginning of our era.

The Four Gospels

The fact remains, though, that we do have the Bible. And it is Scripture rather than the historical references to Jesus in other documents that provides our primary information about history's central figure. Specifically, there are four Gospels (Matthew, Mark, Luke, and John) that claim to give us a true account of the life, teachings, and abiding significance of Jesus of Nazareth.

Although the Gospels are sometimes called "biographies," they do not really fit that literary category. There is no personal description of Jesus, very little is said of his youth, and nothing is told of his formative pre-adult years at Nazareth. By the estimate of one New Testament scholar, all the material in the four Gospels covers a total of no more than forty days out of Jesus' life.

It is probably best to think of the Gospels as "tracts" designed to create faith among non-Christians and to confirm the faith of Christians. The third Gospel is addressed to a nobleman named Theophilus and presents itself as an "orderly account" of the life of Jesus (Luke 1:1–4). Whereas both Mark and Luke were not personally involved in the events of Jesus' life and had to draw on eyewitness accounts and research into documents already produced about Jesus, Matthew and John wrote their Gospels from the perspective of participants. In John's own words, he wrote to produce faith "that Jesus is the Christ" with the assurance that such faith would lead converts to "life in his name" (John 20:31).

The Gospel According to Matthew was written by one of Jesus' apostles, also called Levi (Matt. 9:9–13; cf. Mark 2:13–17; Luke 5:27–32). It was likely written sometime between A.D. 60 and 70. It is very Jewish in tone and presents Jesus as the realization of Israel's messianic hope. Its purpose is to portray Jesus of Nazareth as king over the kingdom of God.

The Gospel According to Mark was written for Gentiles by a Jew. It does not assume the knowledge of the Old Testament that Matthew does and typically explains Jewish language and customs for non-Jewish readers. It was composed by a trusted associate of Peter (cf. 1 Peter 5:13) and likely draws heavily on the teachings and personal recollections of that apostle. Justin Martyr quotes this Gospel in the second century and calls it the "memoirs of Peter." It presents Jesus as the Suffering Servant of God. Its depiction of Jesus as a man of action—serving others and willing to die for them—would have had a powerful appeal to the Roman mind of the time.

The Gospel According to Luke is unique among the Gospels. It is the only one written by a Greek. It and its companion volume, Acts of the Apostles, were written during the two years their author was at Rome with Paul during the apostle's imprisonment from A.D. 60–62 (Col. 4:10–17; Philem. 24). Written by a Greek for other Greeks, it is concerned to show that the Jewish Messiah is the Savior of all humanity.

The Gospel According to John was written in the latter years of the life of one of Jesus' original apostles. Probably prepared around A.D. 90–95, it was intended for both Jews and Gentiles. Its concern was to develop the theme of new life in Jesus Christ. This "disciple whom Jesus loved" (John 21:20; cf. Mark 5:37) was eager to let all people know of the difference made in human lives by the presence and power of the one he confessed as the Son of God.

Admittedly these documents were written by people who believed the claims of the one about whom they were writing. This fact does not make them unacceptable as historical evidence about Jesus. As we have seen already, the New Testament materials in general and the Gospels in particular have been demonstrated to be reliable sources of historical data.

These four tracts about Jesus have a ring of authenticity about them. They tell of great crowds, miracles, sermons, and admiring disciples. They also tell of people who charged Jesus with demon possession and with being an illegitimate child. They record the accounts of disciples who fled under threat and of one apostle who turned defector. They tell of a humiliating death at the hands of the Romans. This is not the way people write when trying to manufacture a person or to perpetuate a hoax.

Honest scholars cannot dismiss the testimony of the Gospels to the life and work of Jesus of Nazareth. As Joseph Klausner, late professor at Hebrew University in Jerusalem analyzed it: "If we had ancient sources like those in the Gospels for the history of Alexander the Great or Julius Caesar for example, we should not cast any doubt on them whatsoever."[12]

Remainder of the New Testament

Other New Testament materials outside the four Gospels add some relevant information about the life of Jesus. Acts of the Apostles gives additional information about post-resurrection appearances of Jesus and his ascension to heaven (Acts 1:1-11). It also records a frequently cited saying of Jesus that is found only in Acts and nowhere in the Gospels: "It is more blessed to give than to receive" (Acts 20:35).

The epistles of Paul give an account of the institution of the memorial supper to Jesus (1 Cor. 11:20–26), discuss several post-resurrection appearances of Jesus (1 Cor. 15:1–8), and often refer to certain features of his personality and work (cf. Phil. 2:5–11).

The general epistles of the New Testament add no new information about the events of Jesus' life. They assume a knowledge of the fundamental facts about him and proceed to build on them. Hebrews, for example, is an extended argument for the superiority of Jesus and his message over Moses and the Law. Three epistles from John warn against people who were teaching false doctrines about Jesus that effectively denied his humanity (cf. 2 John 7).

The Book of Revelation closes the New Testament canon and shows the glory and concerns of the risen Christ. He is presented as being alive from the dead, exalted at the right hand of the Father, and supervising the welfare of his people on Earth.

In the pages to follow, we will use these biblical sources in two ways. First, we will use them as accredited sources of information about the life, teachings, claims, and historical circumstances of Jesus Christ. We will not beg the question of his deity or reason in a circle by using the assertions of Scripture as proof of their truthfulness. But we will look to the Bible—based on the foundation of the previous four chapters of this book—to establish his claims, to examine the evidence relevant to those claims, and to substantiate the reaction of both friends and foes to his deeds. Second, we will use Scripture to clarify the significance of certain events in Jesus' life and to establish the extent of the demands he makes on human beings who would be his disciples today.

This use of Scripture must be allowed merely to discuss Jesus of Nazareth, since it consists of the primary historical documents about him. By analogy, think of what happens in a courtroom. The defendant is allowed to testify on his own behalf, to make whatever claims he wishes, and to call as many witnesses as he chooses. But both the defendant and his witnesses are subject to intensive scrutiny and cross-examination. So it must be with Jesus and the Bible.

The Christian apologist invokes the right to offer Jesus and to present the evidence about him contained in the Bible. Yet he must also be willing to have those claims and their supporting statements subject to critical testing. Truthful claims have nothing to fear from close analysis.

Ultimately the doctrine of the deity of Christ cannot be argued apart from considerations of the Bible's inspiration, infallibility, and authority. This is why the sequence of topics in *Prepare to Answer* was laid out in a pattern that moved from epistemology to theism to Scripture to Jesus.

Jesus' Impact on History

In the most general of terms, one begins to take notice of Jesus because of the impact he has had on the course of human history. It is not an exaggeration to say that *the greatest miracle associated with the Christian religion is the person of Jesus Christ and the impact he has had on the human race.*

The writer and historian H. G. Wells, who was himself an unbeliever in terms of his personal attitude toward Jesus' deity, expressed an opinion of him that few historians would oppose.: "When I was asked which single individual has left the most permanent impression on the world, the manner of the questioner almost carried the implication that it was Jesus of Nazareth. I agreed."[13]

Many people have observed the amazing parallels in the lives of Socrates and Jesus of Nazareth. Both were committed to the improvement of the souls of men. Each gathered a band of disciples about him and taught them extensively. Both alienated the Establishment of their time. And both died by virtue of injustice.

When Socrates died, however, Athens and the world were largely unchanged. His words were forgotten except by a few students. Today he may be studied briefly by college students in a world literature or humanities course. Then he fades from memory and slips back into obscurity.

When Jesus died, the whole world was affected and will never be the same again. His words are quoted, written about, and lived by in all corners of the world—including countries that consciously attempt to keep his influence out. More books have been written about Jesus than any other person in history. His vision of God, truth, and love is the foundation upon which millions conduct their life affairs every day.

A few devoted disciples of Socrates were willing to suffer ridicule for their allegiance to him. Peter, James, Paul, and many others have not only suffered but also have been willing to die rather than deny Jesus as their Lord. Socrates was a great man, but *only* a man. Jesus Christ was Immanuel, God with us.

An anonymous tribute to the magnetism of Jesus over the centuries circulates in slightly different forms. It captures the essence of this point about his impact on history so well that it deserves to be quoted here.

Born in an obscure village, he was the child of a peasant woman. Growing up in another out-of-the-way and disdained village, he worked in a carpenter shop until he was about 30. Then, for three years, he was an itinerant preacher who both talked and listened. He helped people whenever he could.

He never wrote a book. He never held an office. He never went to college. He never had a family of his own or owned a home. He never traveled over 200 miles from the place where he was born.

He never did any of the things that usually accompany greatness and had no credentials but himself.

While he was still a young man, the tide of public opinion turned against him. His friends ran away. He was turned over to his enemies. He went through a mockery of a trial, after which he was executed along with two thieves. While he was dying, his executioners gambled for the only piece of property he owned—a coat. Only because a generous friend offered his own cemetery plot was there a place for him to be buried.

Nineteen centuries have now come and gone, and today he is the central figure of the human race. The leader of the column of spiritual progress. The ultimate example of love.

It is no exaggeration to say that all the armies that ever marched, all the navies that ever sailed, all the kings who have ever reigned, all the congresses that have ever convened, put together, have not affected the life of man upon this Earth as that One Solitary Life.

In the light of his supernatural person and influence, all the other miracles attributed to Jesus are credible. Divorced from such a personality, even the report of such things could hardly have survived. History has no record of anyone else whose every utterance and deed have the ring of truth to so many hearts. There has been only one Jesus of Nazareth, and his influence is best explained in terms of the biblical claim that he is divine.

Jesus' Personal Sinlessness

The mark Jesus left on history rests largely on the character he exhibited. His personal perfection lets us know that he was no ordinary mortal with a high IQ and sense of civic responsibility.

If God were to take human form and come among his human creatures, what sort of character would you expect to see? He would surely demonstrate the type of character

Jesus of Nazareth displayed. He would be without sin himself and would be made indignant by sin around him, but he would be compassionate toward the victims of sin. Could the life of Jesus be described more succinctly?

Yes, you would expect his loyal disciples such as Peter (1 Peter 1:19; 2:22) and John (1 John 3:5) to testify to his unblemished character. But think about the unusual case of Judas Iscariot, a disciple who turned against Jesus for reasons that are not fully clear to us. When Judas struck a bargain with the people plotting against Jesus, it would have been devastating for this insider to point to Christ's secret sins or to expose the miracles of his ministry as tricks. But, as a matter of fact, the worst he could do for the thirty pieces of silver he was paid was to lead Jesus' enemies to the place where he was praying.

The Roman official who had charge over the trial and eventual execution of Jesus was Pontius Pilate. On receiving his prisoner and after investigating the charges that had been brought against him, Pilate's verdict was that the accused man was innocent. His words to the people determined to see Jesus put to death were: "I have examined him in your presence and have found no basis for your charges against him" (Luke 23:14). It was the political pressure exerted on Pilate rather than crimes committed by his prisoner that led to Jesus' crucifixion.

Yet there was no trace of smugness or self-righteousness about the Nazarene. He made no compromise with evil, but he never turned away anyone who sought his aid in dealing with sin. Jesus hated sin but loved the people who were captive to it.

He ate with people who were outcasts to the religious aristocracy (Luke 15:1–2). He subjected himself to the criticisms of others by letting sinners touch him (Luke 7:36–39) and by visiting in the home of a hated tax collector (Luke 19:1–9). He showed compassion to a woman caught in the act of adultery and encouraged her to leave her immoral ways (John 7:53–8:11). On these occasions, when the Pharisees and teachers of the Law chided Jesus for being in company with known sinners, even then they did not accuse him of participating in their sins. There is simply no fault to be found in the moral character of Jesus Christ.

God, walking among his human creatures, would have dealt with sin exactly as Jesus of Nazareth dealt with it. His character is therefore fully consistent with his claims.

Conclusion

To believe in God because of arguments, proofs, and rationally adequate responses to the critics of theism will hardly be enough for most of us. Does it matter whether there is a God in heaven if he doesn't know me? What difference does his presence "beyond the starry skies" make to a tormented, guilty conscience? What is that God to someone who is lonely, abused, pregnant at fifteen, or sleeping on the streets?

But suppose that someone explains to me that God is not merely the name of a divine being discovered at the end of a successful philosophic proof but a caring, merciful, and warmhearted person who knows my situation. More than that, he entered into the human situation. He gave up the privileged status of deity enthroned in heaven to become a real man who would live among other men and women.

The Christian faith holds that God came among us with a human face. That face was no mere mask, no pretense, no mockery of our predicament. It was a full identification with us in our fallenness so that we might know the fullness of his love for us.

If Jesus of Nazareth is who he claimed to be, then God does know about us. More than that, he *knows* us, and this God of the cosmos has offered himself to us at a personal level. If this can be proved true, then nothing can ever be the same again for the one who believes it.

10

I Confess—He's the One!

Chapter 9 focused most of its attention on nonbiblical data that relates to the historicity of Jesus of Nazareth. Although some would rush past all that evidence and proceed directly to the biblical material, we have taken the time to walk through it with some care. "It is the gospel—the Good News of Jesus' atoning death—that is the basis of Christian hope," comes the impatient response of a zealous believer, "not some Roman or Jewish testimony about the historicity or character of the man Jesus."

Of course, the *gospel* is the critical issue about Christ. And, of course, the central documents of relevance to the gospel's testimony to him are the New Testament materials. They explain who Jesus is, why he came among men, and the response humans are expected to make to him. But the *who* and *why* of Jesus and the *response* we should make to him must not be separated from the facts of history.

If the facts are dubious or false, there is no gospel. It is Scripture that tells how Jesus and the events of his life, death, and resurrection constitute a divine revelation and stand as the foundation for redemption. Yet there is simply no credibility to the claim that these events of history are revelatory and redemptive if the events themselves are in doubt.

The crossing of the Red Sea by Israel reveals nothing about God if the event itself never took place. The deliverance of Daniel from the jaws of ravenous lions proves nothing about God's care for his people if such an event never happened. And if Jesus was not a real figure of history, if he did not really live and die under the circumstances related in Scripture and if he did not rise bodily from the grave, there is no gospel to preach.

Our proclamation of Jesus cannot be divorced from historical fact, historical and scientific research, and the pointed questions that skeptics have raised. We must have the honesty and courage to say: "If the facts of history falsify the message we preach, we want to know it. We want to teach only what is true." Precisely because the message *is* true, believers can allow it to be tested in the crucible of honest inquiry. The unbeliever who does not see this sort of integrity with the gospel message will be prejudiced against it from the start.

The previous chapter, then, was a summary of history's witness to what God has done through Jesus. That testimony is weighty, significant, and impressive. But, *in order* to claim that Jesus of Nazareth is the Son of God, more is necessary. We are in something of the same position here as earlier when studying the inspiration of Scripture: external evidences about the Bible's historical accuracy are necessary to a case for inspiration, but they are not sufficient to establish it. In the case of Jesus of Nazareth, the information about his historicity, personal character, and far-reaching impact on history may be considered as necessary evidences of his deity but are insufficient of themselves to prove it.

In this chapter, we turn to the unique things about Jesus that set him apart from all others. We concentrate our attention on the type of evidence that is sufficient to justify the claims Jesus made to be God among men. Specifically, attention will be given to predictive prophecy and miracles. Against the background of what was established in chapter 6 about biblical prophecies concerning future events, it will be demonstrated that Jesus of Nazareth fulfills a unique expectation that was created over the centuries for him. Then we will focus on the apologetic value of miracles in general to the authentication of Jesus' claims for himself, with particular attention being given to the virgin conception and bodily resurrection.

There is a very real sense in which this chapter must be seen as the crescendo to *Prepare to Answer*. Everything that has gone before becomes prelude now to the issue of personal faith in Jesus Christ as Messiah, Son of God, and Redeemer.

Predictive Prophecy

Practically every civilization in antiquity had a "circular view" of history. That is, people such as the Egyptians and Babylonians held that all things repeat themselves in unending cycles. With this view of things, history is without either vision or purpose. To the contrary, however, the Jewish perception of history was "linear" in nature. Thus, the Old Testament regards history as teleological rather than cyclical, moving toward a goal rather than simply unfolding without meaning.

More specifically still, the writers of the Old Testament believed that God was working in history to bring "the kingdom of God" among men. This great, climactic event was to be accomplished through the work of a figure they called the Messiah, the Anointed One. As they anticipated the coming of God's Anointed One who would usher in heaven's kingdom reign on Earth, a great body of literature was produced. As these men wrote of Tyre and Nineveh, they also wrote of Messiah and his kingdom. The unfailing fulfillment of the predictions about the former became Israel's confident ground of expectation about the latter's coming true as well.

The argument for the deity of Jesus Christ based on these predictions in Scripture was not invented recently by Christians. As outlined above, it rests on the ancient expectations of the Jews. Before Jesus was born, students of Hebrew Scripture had built up a mass of literature containing the predictions that Christians now allege to be fulfilled in Christ. Prophecy lists about the Messiah have been found at Qumran, for example, showing that serious students of the sacred texts were compiling key statements from Moses, David, Isaiah, and others. His tribe, the city where he would be born, the startling reaction of people to his presence, and other features of his career were all predicted—hundreds of years before the time of Jesus.

The argument for Jesus' deity based on these predictive prophecies has been used from his own day to the present. "If you believed Moses, you would believe me," Jesus once told his hearers, "for he wrote about me" (John 5:46; cf. Luke 24:25–27). Paul insisted that the key to interpreting the entire Old Testament is Jesus Christ. He claimed that something of a "veil" obscures one's understanding of Scripture if Jesus is excluded from the interpretive process (2 Cor. 3:14-17). And Matthew's Gospel is built around the motif of prediction and fulfillment. Its recurring theme is: "All this took place to fulfill what the Lord had said through the prophet . . . " (cf. Matt. 1:1–16; 2:15, 17, 23; 4:14; 8:17; 12:17, *et al.*).

The Messiah's *lineage* is staked out as Old Testament history unfolds. He would be a descendant of Shem (Gen. 9:26), Abraham (Gen. 12:3), Isaac (Gen. 21:12), Jacob (Gen. 28:14), Judah (Gen. 49:10), and David (2 Sam. 7:16). In the two genealogies given for Jesus in Scripture (Matthew appears to give Jesus' *legal* lineage through Joseph [Matt. 1:1ff], and Luke cites his *maternal* ancestry [Luke 3:23-31]) it is conspicuous that his family tree satisfies the requirements.

The *birthplace* of the Anointed One of Israel was foretold by the prophet Micah (Mic. 5:2). The biblical scholars in the court of Herod the Great knew this prediction (cf. Matt. 2:3–6). The same prophecy was apparently known widely, for some of Jesus' critics who assumed that his birthplace was his boyhood home of Nazareth tried to use this prophecy against him (John 7:42). The fact is, of course, that Jesus was born in Bethlehem (Matt. 2:1–6).

The *unique messenger* who would come to prepare the way for Jesus was also predicted at Malachi 3:1. Later Malachi called this forerunner "Elijah" (Mal. 4:5–6). The people who read this prediction never expected Elijah to return in person. This seems clear from the fact that some people who followed Jesus' ministry considered *him* to be its fulfillment (cf. Matt. 16:14). They understood the prophecy to mean that someone would come "in the spirit and power of Elijah" to precede the Messiah's appearance (Luke 1:17), and John the Baptist fulfilled this prediction in his ministry .

As a matter of fact, the listing of such predictions and their fulfillments could go on almost indefinitely. Messiah's unique triple role as prophet (Deut. 18:15–18; cf. Acts 3:22), priest (Ps. 110; cf. Heb. 5:4–6; 7:1–12), and king (Gen. 49:10; cf. John 18:36). His offer of salvation to Gentiles as well as Jews (Isa. 2:2–3; Zech. 9:10; cf. Gal. 3:28). It is not difficult to find extensive lists of these predictions and their fulfillments, which have been compiled by apologists over the years.

Isaiah 53

One of the most astonishing predictive prophecies about the Messiah is found at *Isaiah 53*. It is put forth here as something of a test case for Old Testament prophecies in general and as a prooftext for the claims of Jesus. It was one of the favorite preaching texts of early Christian evangelists (cf. Acts 8:26–39) and is a detailed description of Yahweh's Suffering Servant who would come to redeem the people of God.

Before reading Isaiah 53 and studying its predictions and their significance for Jesus' claims, one should first observe that this text is capable of satisfying the tests of a genuine biblical prediction (which were outlined in chapter 6 of this book). The prophetic chapter in question undeniably antedates the time of Jesus by several hundred years[1] and deals with events that could not have been discerned or artificially contrived by the author. It is specific in its details and cannot be dismissed on the basis of vagueness or ambiguity. And the fulfillment of the chapter is unequivocal in every particular. The relatively short chapter in question contains at least ten predictive prophecies which are realized in Jesus of Nazareth.[2]

1. Verse one predicts that the Servant will be rejected and that his message will be met with disbelief. The fulfillment of this prediction may be seen in events such as the ones related in John 12:37–43.

2. Verse two anticipates some of the reasons that would underlie his initial rejection by the people of Israel. The fact that Jesus was a peasant from an unpromising place who lacked physical "beauty" or royal "majesty" to attract followers did contribute to prejudices against him and his ultimate rejection by many. Take, as a case in point, Nathanael's early reaction to Jesus based on his background. "Nazareth!" he scoffed. "Can anything good come from there?" (John 1:46).

3. Verse three has him "despised and rejected by men, a man of sorrows, and familiar with suffering." The satisfaction of this part of the prophecy is so generally known as to need no comment (cf. Luke 18:31–32).

4. Verses 4–5, 9b, and 12b indicate that he was to bear the sins of others although he was personally guiltless before God. The New Testament writers claim that the death of Jesus was a vicarious death of the Righteous One for the sinful multitude. This claim is, in fact, at the very heart of the Christian gospel (cf. 2 Cor. 5:21).

5. Verse six sets forth the Suffering Servant as the instrument for calling Yahweh's straying sheep back into the fold. Jesus used this very same representation of his mission in John 10, and his treatment of fallen men and women is best viewed on the model of a shepherd and his straying sheep.

6. Verse seven has the Servant enduring his suffering in silence. He would be bullied and terrorized by his enemies, but he would not resist their evil deeds. This is exactly what happened on the night of Jesus' betrayal and

during the later hours of his trials and execution (Matt. 26:60–63; 27:12–14; Mark 14:60–61).

7. Verse eight predicts that oppressive and unjust proceedings would deny justice to the Servant. The series of "trials" to which Jesus was subjected before Jewish and Roman officials were mockeries of the law and affronts to human decency.

8. Verse nine predicts that the Suffering Servant would be "assigned a grave with the wicked." The crucifixion of Jesus along with two criminals fulfilled this unlikely prediction (Luke 23:32).

9. The same ninth verse also holds forth the seemingly contradictory prospect that the Servant would be "with the rich in his death." This part of the prediction was performed in Jesus' burial in the tomb of the rich Joseph of Arimathea (Matt. 27:57–60).

10. Though crushed and cut off from the living, the chapter closes with the prediction that the Servant would "see his offspring and prolong his days"(v. 10) and receive "a portion among the great" (v. 12). Nothing short of the resurrection, ascension, and exaltation of Jesus must have been in view in these statements.

The total apologetic value of Isaiah 53 argues powerfully both for the inspiration of the book that contains such supernatural prophecies and for the identity of the person who is their fulfillment.

The Miracles of Jesus

Then there are the miracles of Jesus. How shall we view them? Did he really do the things attributed to him in the Gospels? What sort of evidence is there to support the claim that he worked miracles? What would be the apologetic value of such feats?

One view of miracles is to rule them out by a presupposition. "Since a miracle would have to violate the laws of nature, and since nature always operates under the laws of science," someone argues, "miracles cannot occur." This attitude of naturalistic philosophy begs the question by assuming the very thing to be proved. There is a serious logical fallacy involved here by virtue of the ambiguity of the term *laws* in the statement above. On the one hand, a law can be a rule laid down by sovereign authority; on the other, it can be a generalized statement of an observed regularity. The former is a prescriptive law, and the latter is a descriptive one. Scientific laws are only descriptive, never prescriptive. One could even argue that scientific laws are simply God's customary ways, while miracles are his unaccustomed ways.

An equally irresponsible view of miracles is that held by some zealous but uninformed believers who see miracles on every page of Scripture and in every event of life. The fact is, miracles are represented in Scripture as uncommon and infrequent. Their evidential value is in part due to their sporadic occurrence. If miracles were spread out uniformly through history, there would be little notion of their being a "sign" of God's presence. With occasional singular exceptions in the biblical record, there seem to have been perhaps four times in history when miracles were clustered: the creation, the time of Moses, the crisis days of Elijah and Elisha, and the ministry of Jesus and the apostles. If miracles accompany and authenticate divine revelation, they are exactly where we would expect them to be.

By definition, we may say that a miracle is an event so unusual in character that it defies explanation as anything other than the intervention of a supernatural power.

An *a priori* rejection of the possibility of such events is a philosophical problem growing out of a particular world view. And the sort of snobbery we sometimes exhibit toward people of centuries ago, which permits them to believe in miracles because they lived at a time of ignorance and superstition, is also is a bit too smug. The Jews were particularly on guard against false miracles (cf. Deut. 13:1–5), and a degree of skepticism prevailed among the people of Palestine at Jesus' time that far surpassed the civ-

ilization of medieval Europe. Joseph, for example, knew
enough biology that he understood where babies came
from, so he assumed immorality rather than parthenogene-
sis when he learned Mary was pregnant (cf. Matt. 1:19–21).

These general considerations aside for the moment, we
tend to go at the issue of Jesus' miracles a bit too abstractly.
Rather than getting bogged down in the philosophical
issue of the possibility of miracles, we tend to forget the
historical fact that *something unusual happened* in connection
with Jesus' ministry. He did extraordinary things that cannot be explained at the level of normal occurrences. While
Jesus' disciples pointed to those events and attributed
them to the power of God, his enemies pointed to the same
events and assigned credit for them to demonic or magical
forces (cf. Mark 3:22). It never occurred to any of his enemies to claim that nothing out of the ordinary had really
happened. They did not expose him as a fraud or persuade
Judas to reveal the secret of his magical tricks. Even the
derogatory references about Jesus in the *Talmud* do not
deny that he really performed miraculous deeds. They
simply continue the charge that he did those things by the
power of evil rather than by the power of God.

Looking at the question historically, it is significant that
there are some thirty-five episodes involving miracles in
the four Gospels. One or two claimed miracles might be
suspect, but Jesus performed many supernatural feats
under a variety of circumstances. The things he did were
inseparably a part of his ministry that served to establish
both his compassion for people and his authority over
them.

The Gospels record Jesus' healing of people afflicted
with fevers (Mark 1:29–31), leprosy (Mark 1:40–42), and
paralysis (Mark 2:1–12). He restored sight to a man who
had been blind from birth (John 9:1–12). He could stop
storms (Luke 8:22–25), multiply food supplies (Mark
6:30–44), and otherwise control nature. He even raised people from the dead (Mark 5:35–43).

These miracles were not performed with ceremony and

display but naturally and with ease. They were executed from high motives and never for selfish gain. They were done publicly so as to invite people to check what had happened. Again, however, Jesus' miracles were not done simply to inspire awe. They were evidences of his love for frightened and hurting people and were designed to give intelligent beings the evidence they would need to conclude: "Rabbi, we know you are a teacher who has come from God. For no one could perform the miraculous signs you are doing if God were not with him" (John 3:2).

If Jesus did not perform miracles, there is no good reason for us to regard his teachings as authoritative. Apart from the miracles that prove him to be a "teacher who has come from God," he is just another great moral philosopher or religious reformer.

The central miracles associated with the life of Jesus Christ are the ones that began and ended his life on Planet Earth: the virgin conception and the bodily resurrection. For some reason, these central miracles seem to embarrass some apologists for the Christian faith. There has been something of a loss of nerve in confronting the unbelieving world with these claims about Jesus. But if the legitimacy of *any* miracle can be granted, why should one think either of these problematic? If one of these is denied, of what value are the others?

The Virgin Conception

One cannot open a copy of the New Testament and get past the first page without encountering the claim that Jesus Christ was born of a virgin. Matthew begins the Gospel placed first in our New Testaments with this narrative (1:18–23):

> This is how the birth of Jesus Christ came about: His mother Mary was pledged to be married to Joseph, but before they came together, *she was found to be with child through the Holy Spirit.* Because Joseph her husband was a righteous man and did not want to expose her to public disgrace, he had in mind to divorce her quietly.

But after he had considered this, an angel of the Lord appeared to him in a dream and said, "Joseph son of David, do not be afraid to take Mary home as your wife, because *what is conceived in her is from the Holy Spirit.* She will give birth to a son, and you are to give him the name Jesus, because he will save his people from their sins."

All this took place to fulfill what the Lord had said through the prophet: "The virgin will be with child and will give birth to a son, and they will call him Immanuel"—which means, "God with us" [italics added].

The third Gospel tells of Mary's pregnancy from her own perspective. Luke 1:30–35 tells how the angel Gabriel appeared to her to help prepare this young girl for the great event that was about to occur in her life:

But the angel said to her, "Do not be afraid, Mary, you have found favor with God. You will be with child and give birth to a son, and you are to give him the name Jesus. He will be great and will be called the Son of the Most High. The Lord God will give him the throne of his father David, and he will reign over the house of Jacob forever; his kingdom will never end."

"How will this be," Mary asked the angel, *"since I am a virgin?"*

The angel answered, "The Holy Spirit will come upon you, and the power of the Most High will overshadow you. *So the holy one to be born will be called the Son of God"* [italics added].

All four Gospels assume the doctrine of the virgin conception. (The term *virgin conception* rather than virgin birth is used throughout this discussion. From all indications, the birth of the child Jesus and his growth to maturity were perfectly normal and ordinary. The single miraculous event connected with his birth was the matter of conception in Mary's womb without intercourse.) Two of the Gospels give details about it. And it is all the more amazing that one of these writers, Luke, was a physician. All his training and experience would compel him to deny the possibility of such an event. Diligent historian that we know Luke was (cf. chapter 5), he must have investigated the matter carefully. Perhaps he even interviewed Mary. Then, when he wrote his account of the life of Jesus, he affirmed that Jesus of Nazareth was born of a virgin.

Seven hundred years before the birth of Jesus, the Holy Spirit had moved the prophet Isaiah to foretell the birth of the Messiah. "Therefore the Lord himself will give you a sign: The virgin will be with child and will give birth to a son . . . " (Isa. 7:14; cf. Matt. 1:22–23).

Isaiah predicted the virgin conception; New Testament writers recorded its occurrence; and it stands as a sign from God as to the identity of Jesus of Nazareth as the Son of God, the long-awaited Messiah, the Savior of the world. If we add this magnificent prediction to the ones already cited in this chapter about the Messiah, we are able to identify with certainty that individual to whom the Old Testament had pointed for centuries.

The New Testament explains how the redemption of sinful humankind depended on a *"mediator"* who could restore fallen men and women to the fellowship of a holy God. To fill that role, a member of the Godhead became a man in order to share our humanity (cf. 1 Tim. 2:5–6). His coming among us was an *incarnation* (a "becoming-in-flesh") by means of his birth by Mary. Whereas normal procreation results in the initiation of a new being, the means chosen for an already-existing divine being to enter flesh was for the Holy Spirit to overshadow Mary and to form his body in her womb.

The credibility of the virgin conception is tied directly to the general credibility of the biblical writers, which has already been established for the Gospels. Matthew and Luke tell of Jesus' birth in the same clear, matter-of-fact way in which they record the other events of his life and ministry. There is nothing defensive in their accounts. There is no trace of embellishment.

Furthermore, there is the behavior of the central characters in the account. When Mary learned of her pregnancy, the first place she went was to the home of Zechariah and Elizabeth (Luke 1:39–40). Since Zechariah was a priest and would have had the obligation to deal with an illegitimate pregnancy with very rigid severity, her willingness to seek out the couple's company testifies to her moral innocence. Joseph's initial reaction to Mary's pregnancy is exactly what we would expect from a decent man who knew he had not fathered the child she was carrying. It is his subsequent kindness to her that makes no sense at all unless the virgin conception was confirmed to him by the miraculous sign recorded in Matthew's Gospel.

Because conception is a private event, there is no way to bring anything but circumstantial evidence to bear on the question of Jesus' conception. There is not the sort of public evidence for a virgin conception that there is for a bodily resurrection. One's ability to believe the doctrine rests ultimately on his or her view of the inspiration of Scripture. If the Bible is accepted as inspired of God and fully true, then one can believe the account. If the Bible is accepted only on those points where some source external to Scripture establishes it, the account of Jesus' birth will have to be rejected.

[Mary] was so completely willing for God to fulfill his purpose that she was ready to risk the stigma of being an unmarried mother, of being thought an adulteress herself and of bearing an illegitimate child. She surrendered her reputation to God's will. I sometimes wonder if the major cause of much theological liberalism is that some scholars care more about their reputation than about God's revelation. Finding it hard to be ridiculed for being naive and credulous enough to believe in miracles, they are tempted to sacrifice God's revelation on the altar of their own respectability. . . . But *of course* critics will smirk and scoff: let them! What matters is that we allow God to be God and to do things his way, even if with Mary we thereby risk losing our good name.[3]

When all has been said on the subject, then, we are left with a dilemma of history. A child was born to Mary and Joseph, and Joseph was not his biological father. Stripping away all the subtleties about his birth, the issue comes down to a choice between believing in the unprecedented miraculous conception of a child in Mary's womb by the Holy Spirit or saying that Jesus of Nazareth was a bastard whose origins were accounted for, by both his mother and the early church, with a preposterous lie.

While granting freely that there is no historical precedent for such a conception and birth to a woman who was still a virgin, neither is there any good reason to think that a God who can speak the cosmos into existence would find any difficulty in bringing about such a birth. The difficulty here is not believing in the virgin conception so much as believing that miracles of *any* sort can happen.

The Bodily Resurrection

When Jesus' enemies asked for a sign of his deity, he offered them only one. It was not the virgin conception, for this was something that could not be confirmed publicly. Nor was it one of his public feats, such as healing the blind or calming a storm, for his enemies had admitted his power to do those things but had attributed that power to Satan. Instead, he pointed to his bodily resurrection, which would come after their rejection of him, his crucifixion, and his burial.

> Then some of the Pharisees and teachers of the law said to him, "Teacher, we want to see a miraculous sign from you."
> He answered, "A wicked and adulterous generation asks for a miraculous sign! But none will be given it except the sign of the prophet Jonah. For as Jonah was three days and three nights in the belly of a huge fish, so the Son of Man will be three days and three nights in the heart of the earth" (Matt. 12:38–40).

Just as Jesus had done *before* the fact, so Paul pointed to the bodily resurrection *after* the fact and said that everything about the Christian faith stands or falls with it. ". . . if Christ has not been raised," he said, "our preaching is useless and so is your faith" (1 Cor. 15:14).

Many men have died on crosses. In 519 B.C., the Persian King Darius crucified three thousand Babylonians. In A.D. 66, the Romans crucified thirty-six hundred Jews and thereby lit the flame of revolt throughout Palestine. By the time order was restored, Roman executioners had run out of wood to make crosses. The mere fact that Jesus died on a cross would not account for his significance to history and the devotion he has engendered among millions of followers. Except for the resurrection, his ministry would have ended and been forgotten, and he would have been merely another martyr to a cause. His claim to be God among men would have been ignored.

Jesus Christ either rose bodily from the tomb, or he did not. The faith of devoted Christians is either genuine and will result in eternal life, or it is a foolish form of self-delusion. It is important to note that the claim that Jesus rose from the dead did not develop gradually over the generations or arise centuries after his time. As was shown earlier in this chapter, it was predicted in the Old Testament Book of Isaiah. The enemies of Jesus had heard him predict his own death and resurrection often enough that they immediately took steps to guard the body after he was crucified. Jewish leaders went to Pilate about the matter, reminding him that Jesus had said, "After three days I will rise again." They requested that the tomb be sealed and guarded against the possibility that "his disciples may come and steal the body and tell the people that he has been raised from the dead . . ." (Matt. 27:62–64).

The claim of Jesus' physical, bodily resurrection first began to be made publicly on Pentecost Day not long after his death. It was a mere fifty-one days after his death that the apostles were standing up in the very city where everything had taken place to claim that he was alive again.

What is the evidence that such a resurrection actually took place?

1. *An Empty Tomb.* Jesus was crucified on the Friday before Passover (April 7) of A.D. 30. He was buried in Joseph of Arimathea's borrowed tomb that afternoon, the tomb was sealed, and a guard was posted. But on the following Sunday morning, the tomb was empty.

2. *An Incredible Explanation of the Empty Tomb.* The soldiers posted on guard claimed that some of Jesus' disciples came and stole the body while they slept (Matt. 28:13). On its face, the story is not believable. Could soldiers sleep so soundly that a group of men could move a huge stone weighing several tons, snatch a corpse, and leave without even one of the guards being roused? Furthermore, if the soldiers were indeed asleep, how would they know what had happened to the body or who had done it? No court accepts someone's testimony as to what happened while he was sound asleep.

3. *Consistent Eyewitness Testimony.* Many witnesses under a variety of circumstances testified to the effect that Jesus rose from the dead. These witnesses include the women who came to the tomb early Sunday morning to anoint his body (Matt. 28:1–10, *et al.*); Mary Magdalene (John 20:11–18); Simon Peter (Luke 24:34; cf. 1 Cor. 15:5); two disciples on the Emmaus Road, one of them unnamed (Luke 24:13–35); ten apostles (John 20:19–25); eleven apostles (John 20:26–29); several disciples while they were fishing (John 21:1–23); over five-hundred people at once (1 Cor. 15:6); his brother James (1 Cor. 15:7), and the eleven apostles on the Mount of Olives near Jerusalem (Luke 24:50–52).

It took more than an empty tomb to convince Jesus' disciples that he was alive. Mary Magdalene found the tomb empty and concluded that the body had been stolen (John 20:2, 13). When she reported the empty tomb to Peter and John, they ran to it but did not assume a resurrection. In fact, as John himself later admitted, "They still did not understand from Scripture that Jesus had to rise from the dead" (John 20:9). It took convincing eyewitness encounters to cause them to believe. They touched him, saw the nailprints, and came to faith over the objection of their own doubts and despair.

4. *Notable Silence of Jesus' Enemies.* Why was there no real challenge to the resurrection claim? If Jesus' enemies had moved and hidden the body, they would have produced it to put a stop to the rumors of resurrection. If there had been any evidence that the disciples had stolen the body, the authorities could have produced it and prosecuted them. If there had been any way to stimulate reasonable doubt of the resurrection claim, Jesus' foes would have seized it.

In the Book of Acts, for example, we note the Jewish authorities enjoining the apostles from preaching the resurrection (Acts 4:17–18; 5:28). They did not, however, offer a public response to it, one purporting to show that the apostles were fabricating a myth. If they had been capable of doing so, they would have discredited or falsified the resurrection report and stopped the Christian religion dead in its tracks. Preaching a resurrected Christ at a place and time wherein it was fully possible to check every piece of evidence and to interrogate every witness, the apostles had nothing to fear from speaking about what they had seen with their own eyes.

5. *Transformed Lives of the Apostles.* Jesus' closest associates were demoralized and scattered in fear when their leader was put to death and buried. By their own admission, they did not expect him to rise again. From Pentecost Day forward, however, their preaching had one central theme: Jesus Christ is alive from the dead. They were cursed, hated, driven out of cities, imprisoned, and tortured because of their claim. Many of them died as martyrs.

Could all this be accounted for on the basis of a conspiracy to spread a lie? From their point of view, there was no reason for them to preach the resurrection except that it had really happened. They had everything to lose and nothing to gain by promoting a false claim. They were taking their lives in their own hands, and their very boldness from Pentecost forward is a powerful testimony to the truthfulness of their message.

6. *The Strange Conversion of Saul of Tarsus*. Once an ardent opponent of the Christian faith, Saul had been personally involved in persecuting believers. But, within three or four years of the founding of the church, he had turned from bitter enemy to passionate advocate.

On his own account of the matter, Saul was converted on the basis of a dramatic and unexpected personal confrontation with the resurrected Christ. On his way to persecute Christians in the city of Damascus, the unthinkable happened. The risen Jesus of Nazareth appeared to Saul, spoke to him, and convinced him that the resurrection story was true (Acts 9:1–22; cf. 22:6–21; 26:4–23). From that day forward, he never looked back. Saul—now Paul—gave up his position in the Jewish faith to become a missionary for Jesus Christ. He was hounded by some of the same people who had formerly been his associates in persecuting Christians. He went to jail, he suffered floggings, and eventually was martyred.

The only power great enough to turn a man like Saul from his original course is truth. From the Damascus Road experience, he learned that the apostles were not apostates and lunatics. He learned that they were right. The meaning of the empty tomb he had heard about became clear, and he realized that Jesus was the Messiah and Son of God.

There is no better-attested fact of ancient history than the resurrection of Jesus of Nazareth.

Conclusion

Who, then, was Jesus of Nazareth?

There is no one like him in the annals of history. He never uttered a word that became obsolete. He had no flaws in his personal character. No poet, no dreamer, or no philosopher ever loved people as Jesus loved them. He exploited none and blessed all.

During Jesus' trial for his life, perjured witnesses could not get their stories straight. Even sullen and disinterested Pilate admitted to the mob that there was no fault in Jesus. Three days after a horrible death, he was alive again. Gloriously alive!

Over the centuries, all the people who have tried hardest to imitate Jesus of Nazareth would admit how faulty their imitations have been. He is the original and singular Son of God. Our Redeemer and Lord. In his very person, he stands as the greatest miracle of the ages. No mere mortal is Jesus—*this man is the Son of God!* No mind but an infinite one could have known what he knew. No heart but an infinite one could have loved as he loved. No benefactor but an infinite one could have given the free gift of eternal life that he offers.

There is no doubt. He is Immanuel.

11

He Is *the* Way to God

"Are you the one who was to come, or should we expect someone else?" (Matt. 11:3). This question was put to Jesus by John the Baptist via some of the Baptizer's disciples. We may wonder whether John's faith was wavering during an imprisonment that would end in his death. Or perhaps he was sending the question only for the sake of the disciples who would meet Jesus and hear his answer. Regardless of the motives underlying it, the question received an unequivocal response.

Both Jesus and the evangelists of the early Christian church answered: *Jesus of Nazareth is the one, and besides him there is no other Savior.*

In that answer lies the offensiveness of the gospel to many people. Ours is a shrinking world, and cultures are no longer isolated from one another. Buddhists, Mohammedans, Hindus, Jews, Christians, Marxists—we are no longer separated by mountains, seas, and oceans. We interact. We visit one another, find points of interest in each other's cultures, and find it increasingly desirable to live in peace with one another. Over the past two decades, there has been a major influx of Eastern people, ideas, and religions into the West. As we work to create political and social rapport, should Christians continue to insist on a transcultural and exclusive role for Jesus Christ? Or do these enlightened times call for a moderation of Christianity's singular claims for him?

The larger Christian community is torn on this point. Quoting Gandhi's "I am a Muslim and a Hindu and a Christian and a Jew," some liberal theologians would say that all religions are equally legitimate paths to God or, if you prefer, to enlightenment. They therefore pursue an ecumenism in which any past perceptions or claims to distinctiveness for Christianity are abandoned in favor of an intermingling of various traditions into a single, harmonious system. On the other hand, however, there are theologians who stand in the historic posture of the Christian religion to call for evangelization among all the cultures and individuals who embrace non-Christian systems.

The drift of our time seems to be decidedly away from the exclusivity of Christ and the gospel. The broad tolerance of our age holds that all religions are right and none is wrong. As an academic discipline, "comparative religion" has come to refer to a field of study that sets world religions side by side as expressions of the same fundamental urge within human consciousness. Accordingly, Christianity is only one religion among many, and Jesus of Nazareth is only one spiritually sensitive mentor among many.

Evangelism is no longer an issue among some mainline Protestant churches. For them, there may be social and political agendas, but there is no agenda for proclaiming personal salvation in the name of Jesus and Jesus alone. The Nazarene's claim that "no one comes to the Father except through me" (John 14:6b) is embarrassing to them, and one would never hear a theologian among them echo Peter's sentiment that " . . . there is no other name under heaven given to men by which we must be saved" (Acts 4:12).

The term for this modern sentiment is "syncretism," which here refers to a blending of beliefs and practices from various religious traditions. It offers a warm welcome to all who will dine at a religious smorgasbord. It proposes

a world in which everyone's cat is gray. W. A. Visser't
Hooft, a former general secretary of the World Council of
Churches, defines syncretism as the view

> . . . that there is no unique revelation in history, that there
> are many different ways to reach the divine reality, that all
> formulations of religious truth or experience are by their
> very nature inadequate expressions of that truth, and that it
> is necessary to harmonize as much as possible all religious
> ideas and experiences, so as to create one universal religion
> for mankind.[1]

In this chapter, the claim will be made that Jesus must be
seen as *the* (not *a*) Son of God—incomparable among all
predecessors who anticipated him or rivals who would
succeed or replace him—and the Redeemer of all persons
who would come to God from any culture. It will be a sup-
portive argument for Jesus' own claim that he is the way to
the Father, that no one can come to the Father except
through him (cf. John 14:6).

A Biblical Response to Syncretism

Visser't Hooft points to two waves of syncretism that
antedated Jesus of Nazareth. Both of them are reflected in
Scripture, and the biblical response to these episodes gives
some very helpful perspective.

First, there was the century before the Babylonian exile.
The nation of Judah was led to embrace deities and religious practices from its idol-worshiping neighbors. King
Manasseh openly embraced several elements of Assyrian
culture. He worshiped Asherah, the "Queen of Heaven"
(2 Kings 21:3a; cf. Jer. 7:18), and placed an Asherah pole in
the temple at Jerusalem (2 Kings 21:7). He worshiped the
sun and stars, offered his own children in sacrifice, and
practiced the occult arts (2 Kings 21:3b–6). He also seems
to have been the one responsible for introducing cult pros-
titutes into temple worship (cf. 2 Kings 23:4–7).

It was precisely for offenses such as these that Judah was carried into captivity. The prophets of the period fought the adoption of these trappings of paganism into Jewish worship. The biblical text makes it clear that Yahweh and his spokesmen were consistently enraged by these elements of syncretism. Each was a departure from the ideal announced by Moses and confirmed by Joshua before the Israelites' possession of their Promised Land. Prior to his death, Moses had warned the people: "When you enter the land the LORD your God is giving you, do not learn to imitate the detestable ways of the nations there" (Deut. 18:9; cf. Jer. 44:1–6).

Second, there was an extended period of syncretism from the time of Alexander the Great, which extended well beyond the time of Jesus. Alexander and his successors, among both the Ptolemies and the Seleucids, pushed Greek culture onto the world. So successful was this process among the Jewish people of the intertestamental period that people not only adopted the language, architecture, and gods of the Greeks, but some males even underwent surgical procedures to reverse their circumcision. This removal of the covenant sign from a Jewish man would accommodate the Greek ideal of an unmarked physical body and would allow him to participate in Greek athletic events in the nude.

So pervasive and threatening did this Hellenizing spirit become that a reactionary movement to it arose. The Maccabean Revolt was a protest and reform movement during the intertestamental period. From this era came the Sadducean party. Syncretistic in outlook, they collaborated with and accommodated to whatever culture held power over their territory. The Pharisees were the traditionalists who held out against these encroachments. This tension between the two sects extended into the time of Christ.

During Jesus' lifetime, the Roman Empire sought to make a place for all the gods and religions of its conquered people. The Pantheon at Rome was a temple dedicated to all the gods, and emperor worship was but another attempt to use the spirit of syncretism for the benefit of uniting a far-flung empire. The attitude of this period toward religion is nowhere better typified than at Athens. When Paul visited there in the middle of the first century, he found that "the city was full of idols" (Acts 17:16).

Jesus did not seek a position of parity with Zeus, Orpheus, and the deities of the Pantheon. Rather, he claimed to have a unique and unshared position, one bearing total and absolute authority. Thus he told his disciples:

> All authority in heaven and on earth has been given to me. Therefore go and make disciples of all nations, baptizing them in the name of the Father and of the Son and of the Holy Spirit, and teaching them to obey everything I have commanded you (Matt. 28:18–20a).

The attitude of Christians toward this spirit of accommodation was clear and consistent:

> For even if there are so-called gods, whether in heaven or on earth (as indeed there are many "gods" and many "lords"), yet for us there is but one God, the Father, from whom all things came and for whom we live; and there is but one Lord, Jesus Christ, through whom all things came and through whom we live (1 Cor. 8:5–6).

Two later periods of syncretism traced by Visser't Hooft are the Renaissance and our contemporary civilization. But there is no better summary of the orthodox Christian view of Jesus than the one quoted by Paul in one of his epistles. The lines are probably from an early Christian hymn.

> Therefore God exalted him to the highest place
> and gave him the name that is above every name,
> that at the name of Jesus every knee should bow,
> in heaven and on earth and under the earth,
> and every tongue confess that Jesus Christ is Lord,
> to the glory of God the Father (Phil. 2:9–11).

The Gospel as Basis for Exclusivity

Gandhi's oft-quoted "I am a Muslim and a Hindu and a Christian and a Jew" is perfectly intelligible as a *Hindu* statement. But it is strikingly un-Muslim, un-Christian, and un-Jewish. While the Hindu religion holds all space-time experience to be "illusion" and glories in relativism and obscurity, the Muslim, Christian, and Jewish religions all claim to be grounded in absolutes. For each of these religions, there is a pronounced "scandal of particularity" in that each claims an unshared allegiance from its devotees.

For Christianity, though, the claim is even more emphatic because it centers on a particular personal claim. Other exclusivistic religions say, "Here is the path to truth. Believe this and you will discover life." By contrast, Jesus says, "*I* am the way and the truth. Believe in *me* and *I* will give you life."

The basis, then, of Christianity's exclusivity is *the person of Jesus of Nazareth*. There is no claim of finality for Christianity in any of its historical expressions. The first-century church at Jerusalem, Antioch, or Corinth was not definitive. No present-day denomination or local church can claim finality for itself. It is only in the person of Jesus Christ that Christianity can claim to be unique among world religions.

The Christian religion is not making just another claim that there has appeared a prophet through whom God has spoken in a significant way. Nor is the claim about a man of such holiness that one catches a sense of the divine by being in his presence. The claim is that Jesus Christ *is* God. He is God among us. He is God saving us. He is God delivering us. The foundation for such a claim is in the historical facts traced in the previous chapter: the birth, death, and resurrection of Jesus of Nazareth.

The significance of the miraculous conception of Jesus in Mary's womb and his birth of a virgin is expressed in the theological term *incarnation*. This is an extraordinary and staggering notion. "The Word became flesh and lived for a while among us," wrote the apostle John. "We have seen his glory, the glory of the One and Only [Son], who came from the Father, full of grace and truth" (John 1:14).

The primary objection to the idea of incarnation seems to be a perfectly natural one: Why would God leave the perfection of heaven to come to Earth? A third-century critic of Christianity expressed his reaction to such a belief this way: "How can one admit that the divine should become an embryo, that after his birth he is put in swaddling clothes, that he is soiled with blood and bile, and worse things yet?"[2]

There is no philosophical argument that makes sense of the incarnation. Christians who think about it deeply cannot really be shocked at the reaction of horror that people may have to such a notion. How many of us seriously think about giving up our homes to go live among the homeless? How many are standing in line to join a leper colony in India to empty the bedpans of the sickest patients? Analogies fail when one seeks to make meaningful a deed that is utterly unprecedented and unique.

The only thing that makes the incarnation coherent at any level is not philosophical argument but love.

> Why did my Savior come to earth,
> And to the humble go?
> Why did he choose a lowly birth?
> Because he loves me so!

Only once in the history of the world has someone come among the human race daring to claim that "whoever has seen me has seen God." The proof he offered was not lofty speeches about metaphysical issues but humble identification with the poorest and guiltiest of the human race. The presentation of his person was not with pageantry but by taking our miseries to himself and washing our feet.

Perhaps critics such as Porphyry and his present-day counterparts will still insist that they could only be impressed with a God who showed himself dramatically and gloriously. With overwhelming logic and irresistable personal presence. In regal elegance. At an intimidating distance from his creatures. Yet Jesus comes and reveals a God who cares about us, shares our frailties, and has compassion for our fallenness.

Precisely because of his love for us, Jesus has refused to stagger us with philosophers' arguments and has chosen instead to offer himself in a manger. Instead of a syllogism, he has given the light of hope in the darkness of human despair. In the place of astonishing logic, he has revealed himself through amazing grace.

Then there is the matter of his death. No one else has made the claims about his own death that Jesus and the apostles have made for *his* death. While there are several theological words that could be chosen to express its meaning, there is probably none clearer and more forceful than "atonement."

Atonement refers to a "making at one" (at-one-ment) and speaks of the process by which a holy God and a sinful human race can be united, reconciled, put at peace. Because God is holy, he can neither participate in nor overlook sin. Because human beings are sinful, we are separated from him. Our relationship has been disrupted and broken. Fallen men and women need a means of access to his divine favor.

Our sin is an insult to God's honor and holiness. Out of his infinite perfection and wisdom, he has given a law that expresses his ideal will for our behavior. It is not the capricious law of a tyrant. It is law rooted in love, law designed to protect us from harm and to enable us for righteousness. But we have defied his law. We are lawbreakers and sinners. God cannot wave his hand and pretend that his law is unimportant or that our sinful behavior does not really matter. So, between the extremes of ignoring our sinful behavior on the one hand and simply abandoning us to our own self-destruction on the other, he chose to take the initiative in dealing with sin.

Heaven took the initiative in relation to sin by means of the death of Jesus of Nazareth. The just penalty for sin is death (Rom. 6:23). Prior to the coming of Jesus, a sinner was allowed to substitute an animal victim to bear the death penalty due for his or her sin. Justice was thereby satisfied and atonement was secured. The shedding of the animal's blood signified that a life had been taken in payment for sin. It had been substituted for the worshiper's own sin-stained life. This was, of course, a symbolic act. There was no inherent value in the sacrifice offered that would satisfy a sin debt. It was only by virtue of grace that a human could substitute a bull or goat on an altar, for there was certainly no equivalence of animal and human life in the divine scheme of things.

The Old Testament doctrine of atonement established the fact that, by divine appointment, "without the shedding of blood there is no forgiveness" (Heb. 9:22b). The New Testament writers took up this theme and related it directly to the death of Jesus. All the sacrifices prior to him were interpreted as pointing forward to Jesus as the perfect "Lamb of God" (John 1:36) who was offered up as the once-for-all sacrifice for sin (Heb. 10:1–18).

The New Testament presents Jesus' death as the means of turning away from sinners the horrible fate we were due. Because of sin's offensive nature, a holy God can only be angered by it and must react justly with his wrath. Yet, because of his love for humans, he sought a way to expend that wrath without consuming the creatures he had made in his own image. It is Jesus' death that has turned away divine wrath from those who believe in him, for he stepped between sinners and the death blow we were due for our deeds. Now, when we look at the cross, we see how greatly God loves us and how truly horrible our sins are.

One of the most beautiful messianic texts of the Old Testament points to this part of the saving work of Jesus:

> But he was pierced for our transgressions,
>   he was crushed for our iniquities;

the punishment that brought us peace was upon him,
and by his wounds we are healed (Isa. 53:5).

Peter reflected this same perspective on the death of Jesus when he wrote: "He himself bore our sins in his body on the tree, so that we might die to sins and live for righteousness; by his wounds you have been healed" (1 Peter 2:24).

This is an unprecedented representation of the divine nature. It is without parallel as a deed assigned to God. Other religions may picture a grieved or angry deity, but none besides Christianity pictures God as coming personally to set the matter right. God himself takes the full force of divine wrath due to sin in order to let sinners go free. It is not that we must see sin as merely illusory or act ourselves to placate an angry deity by our good works. Rather, God offers himself as the sinners' substitute and pays the full debt that was owed as the penalty for sin.

The atoning death of Jesus not only allows but also requires an exclusive claim about him as Savior. If his saving work was to teach or model a lifestyle, the claim could be made with plausibility that others could teach and model it also. Because his saving work is the personal act of dying as the perfect Lamb of God, his work is unshared and inimitable.

Then we come face to face again with the resurrection. The theological term for its significance is "exaltation." Just as Jesus' birth of a virgin and his death for others are unique, so is his resurrection distinctive.

When examining the biblical record, one might be prone to view the resurrection claim of Jesus as only one among several. After all, were not Jairus's daughter, Lazarus, and a few other individuals alleged to have had the same experience? *No.* At best, the restoration to life of Lazarus and the others is properly termed a "revivification" or "resuscitation." Those recalled from the dead by Jesus, Peter, or Paul were called back only temporarily. They were returned to life only to have to die again.

Jesus was raised from the dead to experience everlasting life, glory, and honor. On the Pentecost Day following soon after his resurrection, Peter declared both that "God has raised this Jesus to life," and that Jesus had been "exalted to the right hand of God" (Acts 2:32–33). Jesus has been exalted "to the highest place" and given "the name that is above every name" (Phil. 2:9). He is the "beginning and firstborn from among the dead" (Col. 1:18). He is "now crowned with glory and honor" (Heb. 2:9).

Following his resurrection, Jesus claimed, "All authority in heaven and on earth has been given to me" (Matt. 28:18). Based on his present exalted position, he saves, forgives sin, and imparts his Holy Spirit (Acts 2:38). Says Paul:

> Since we have now been justified by his blood, how much more shall we be saved from God's wrath through him! For if, when we were God's enemies, we were reconciled to him through the death of his Son, how much more, having been reconciled, shall we be saved through his life! (Rom. 5:9–10).

This text affirms that Jesus Christ is bringing to completion in his resurrected glory the salvation he began for us in his death. As the *living* Lord over his people, he has a role very different from that of "Lord Krishna" to a Hindu or "Lord Buddha" to the Buddhist. There is a present, abiding relationship between Jesus Christ and his people that cannot exist—and is not claimed—between any other proffered savior and his or her devotees.

By his resurrection, Jesus proclaims triumph over sin, darkness, and death. It is a personal triumph. Yet it is much more than that. It is a victory over those same powers to all who believe in him.

Before death can be understood as anything else, it must first be seen for what it is in common perception: Satan's ultimate weapon of terror against the human race. Since death is in time, its coming is irreversible. People try to postpone it, evade it, cheat it, avoid it. By running from the reality of death, we only flee reality. No one avoids death.

"Do not be afraid. I am the First and the Last," says the resurrected Christ. "I am the Living One; I was dead and behold I am alive for ever and ever! And I hold the keys of death and Hades" (Rev. 1:17b–18). According to Scripture, Jesus died and rose again that he might "destroy him who holds the power of death—that is, the devil—and free those who all their lives were held in slavery by their fear of death" (Heb. 2:14b–15). This, too, is the meaning of the resurrection and is unique to the Christian religion.

Satan had held the race in bondage to the fear of death long enough. Jesus faced him at the cross, appeared to have been defeated at the tomb, but burst forth in victory on the morning of the resurrection. Jesus now shouts at death to ask: "Where is your sting? Where is your victory?" He crushed Satan. Disarmed him. Took the keys of death and Hades from him. Thus, the resurrection affirms to Christians that Satan's worst is not enough to destroy them. As he did with the resurrection of Jesus, God will have the final word. Life will triumph over death. Right over wrong. Good over evil. Truth over lies. God over Satan.

There is, then, a very real scandal of particularity about Jesus. One must ultimately believe that he is either everything or nothing, Lord or weirdo, Savior of all or savior of none. With such great and exclusive claims as are made for him, we may at first be stunned. But, understanding the meaning of his birth, death, and resurrection, any lesser claim would be trite and unworthy.

Conclusion

This book began with an investigation of the nature of faith. It has offered the framework for a rational faith in the God of the Bible. At the end, however, we have come to an awareness of the God who has sought us in Jesus. We have not found God. He has found us.

In our human activity of seeking truth, we have walked
the path of honest inquiry. As we were searching for God,
we discovered that he had long before been searching for
us. Now we find that salvation is in Christ and in him
alone—not by our work of intellectual probing or by any
other work we have done but by his grace.

12

Why People Reject Christianity

God created human beings with minds, and he expects us to use them. Jesus taught, engaged in argument, answered critics' questions, and otherwise fought the battle for the minds of men. He sought no shallow emotional commitment but a committed discipleship founded on informed faith.

Whenever Christians are faithful to their calling, they battle in Jesus' name for the minds of men. Paul reminds us that "The weapons we fight with are not the weapons of the world. On the contrary, they have divine power to tear down strongholds. We demolish arguments and every pretension that sets itself up against the knowledge of God, and we take captive every thought to make it obedient to Christ" (2 Cor. 10:4–5).

This book has been an attempt to address some of the intellectual issues involved with Christian faith. It has made an affirmative case for the central tenets of theism, the inspiration of the Bible, and the deity of Jesus Christ. Along the way, several objections have been faced—with the dual task of trying to reinforce faith among believers and to offer evidence to unbelievers that would appeal to their rationality.

Strife and contention are negative qualities, and Christians are not to indulge in verbal fisticuffs of that sort (cf. Titus 3:9). Such contests arise from human pride and are driven by the desire to win at debate; they produce flaring tempers, hurt feelings, and closed doors.

The presentation and defense of the Christian faith must never be allowed to degenerate into verbal sleight of hand. The Christian has a power greater than logic with which to press his case—the power of love. In a classic article on Socrates, a respected Plato scholar points to a fundamental contrast between the "gadfly of Athens" and Jesus of Nazareth that should be kept in mind.

> Jesus wept for Jerusalem. Socrates warns Athens, scolds, exhorts it, condemns it. But he has no tears for it. One wonders if Plato, who raged against Athens, did not love it more in his rage and hate than ever did Socrates in his sad and good-tempered rebukes. One feels there is a last zone of frigidity in the soul of the great erotic; had he loved his fellows more, he could hardly have laid on them the burdens of his 'despotic logic,' impossible to be borne.[1]

Against any Socratic tendency toward "despotic logic," those who attempt Christian apologetics would be better advised to employ more lightning and less thunder, more honesty and less dogmatism, more love and less acrimony.

A New Testament word that refers to the intellectual discipline of searching with a determination to find truth is *dialegomai*. Paul "reasoned with" (NIV) or "argued with" (ASV) the Jews of Thessalonica about the messiahship of Jesus of Nazareth (Acts 17:2). He engaged in the same process of reasoning in his attempt to persuade people of his case among the Corinthians (Acts 18:4), with the people of Ephesus (Acts 18:19), and in other places.

While Paul was in Athens, the hometown of Socrates, he "reasoned [Gk, *dialegomai*] in the synagogue with the Jews and the God-fearing Greeks, as well as in the marketplace day by day with those who happened to be there" (Acts 17:17). Writing on this verse, one evangelical has said:

For the way that Paul addressed the people in the market place Luke uses a distinctive word. He tells us that Paul 'argued.' And lest we fail to appreciate the significance of this, we should note there is here no isolated example of Paul presenting his case in this manner. Not only does Luke frequently use the word 'argue' of his evangelistic ministry, but he also has other words of similar meaning such as 'confound,' 'prove' (Acts 9:22; 17:3), 'dispute' (Acts 9:29), 'powerfully confute' (Acts 18:28). Expressions like this can leave us in no doubt about Paul's normal aim which was to convince people's minds of the truth of the Gospel as means of persuading them to submit their wills.[2]

God does not despise the human mind that he created. He appeals to it through facts, proofs, and reason. "God's way is not to by-pass the understanding, but to enlighten it."[3] This enlightenment does not come from philosophical speculation and semantic chicanery but from an authenticated divine revelation, the authoritative Word of God.

But believers have increasingly withdrawn from the marketplace of dialogue into the safe confines of church buildings. There is very little battling for the minds of men. The field of battle has been abandoned. Thus, there is a great deal of unbelief that relates to factors other than strictly rational processes. It is not that responsible Christian apologists have attempted a case for faith and failed. Rather, there has been a wholesale pullback from the fray and a failure to demonstrate the practicality of Christian faith, each of which stands responsible for much of the rejection of Christianity we witness in our world. In this chapter, we shall examine these two elements and their respective contribution to unbelief. Then we will turn attention to the biblical mandate Christians have for an aggressive presentation of the case for faith that Christians bear.

The Drift to Secularism

One of the nonrational influences that has inclined many to unbelief is the pervasive influence of contemporary secularism.

As defined in the *Oxford English Dictionary*, "secularism" is the notion that morality should be based solely on regard for the well-being of mankind in this present life, to the exclusion of all considerations related to belief in God or a future life. This viewpoint is a conscious and deliberate rejection of the Christian world view and has become something of a new religion in itself. It now dominates Western society.

Secular humanism makes man the norm of all truth and value. It ridicules the idea of a transcendent deity or an eternal and absolute standard of morality. One can cite entertainers, educators, legislators, scientists, theologians(!), writers—people from all spheres of influence—who are aggressive advocates of the nontheistic perspective on life. The foundations of our culture have been shaken by their combined leadership, and they will carry the day completely unless competently trained and passionately committed Christians challenge them. Yet the beliefs and values of secularism are rarely offered for debate. Instead, they are fast coming to be the general axioms of our society through cultural osmosis.

In an interesting article in a magazine devoted to advocating the secularist point of view, direct confrontation with "religionists" is counseled against. The fear is that there are still enough vestiges of faith around that a confrontational approach would be counterproductive, that such an approach "invites automatic hostility from a huge portion of our population."[4] Rather than headlong challenge, the article suggests that the approach of Carl Sagan's *Cosmos* or Jacob Bronowski's *The Ascent of Man* is preferable. That method treats religion "with humor, satire, and a light touch."[5]

The preferred outlets for secularism are not dry lectures and boring books. They include, but are not limited to, such vehicles as children's cartoons, plays, TV sitcoms, movies, and the like. The message is communicated subtly but powerfully when these artistic media are used to promote relativism in thought, values, and behavior. The same media either pretend that religion is a nonentity in Western culture or present it under its most unflattering caricatures.

The beliefs and commitments of a secular world view have been stated rather clearly. Influential persons who are committed to them have published documents that amount to secular versions of a religious creed. The most significant of such creeds are "Humanist Manifesto I" (1933), "Humanist Manifesto II" (1973), and "A Secular Humanist Declaration" (1980).[6]

These publications speak of theism as "an unproved and an outmoded faith." Their authors and signers declare they "can discover no divine purpose of providence for the human species. . . . No deity will save us; we must save ourselves." They flatly assert that the realm of the supernatural is nonsensical and should be abandoned as a significant category among intellectuals. They declare that the human race is the product of nature rather than God and insist that humanity must define all value and meaning in relation to itself rather than deity, Scripture, or any transcendent value.

Some of the best-known personalities of their time signed one or more of these secularist declarations: John Dewey, Isaac Asimov, Antony Flew, B. F. Skinner, A. J. Ayer, Joseph Fletcher, Betty Friedan, Julian Huxley, and others. In every sphere of human achievement, these and similar advocates of unbelief have reshaped the human agenda to their end. Asimov dismisses the traditional Christian position through science fiction, Skinner through psychology, Sagan through books and TV, and so on.

There are encouraging signs, on the eve of the twenty-first century, of a growing disillusionment with the religion of antireligion. Fewer and fewer people are willing to accept the notion that what we call mind, personality, or spirit is merely a fascinating "perking off of consciousness" from our brain cells. Talk of God, the human spirit, and life after death has surfaced again in serious philosophical journals, at the office, and in social gatherings.

There appears to be an emerging determination to seek

out the sacred. A world that has pushed God out of its intellectual, artistic, social, political, and ethical life to the degree ours has is a world resisting one of the most natural instincts of the human heart. Created in the image of God, there is a restlessness about the human spirit when impulses to the divine are denied. The Spanish philosopher Unamuno spoke of what he called "God-ache" in the hearts of unhappy and bewildered people. That term may well be the most appropriate to describe what ails a culture that has drifted so far into secularism. It has God-ache because it has divorced itself from its Creator. Things will get better only as people turn back to God in faith.

As this book has argued, God is not really far from any of us. He shows himself through the creation. His power, majesty, and wisdom are in evidence all around us. More than that, he has spoken to us through prophets and apostles to mark the path of righteousness, life, and hope. Finally, he has showed himself in human form in the person of Jesus Christ.

A world so confused as this one will not find its way through Buddhism, Transcendental Meditation, or the New Age movement. Delving into alleged previous lives, heightened self-awareness, and so-called cosmic consciousness are poor alternatives to the factual base of the Christian religion and its invitation to critical investigation.

All this means that the time is right for a bold initiative by Christian apologists. A secular world that has lost its way needs the positive direction offered by Jesus Christ. But before we turn to the biblical mandate for the apologetic enterprise, there is a second item favoring unbelief that must be noted.

Practical Failures of Christianity

Many people have rejected Christianity because they have never seen a down-to-earth demonstration that the religion of Jesus Christ meets their basic needs. They know the church only under a stereotype. They see it as "big business in vestments." They see it as an isolated and irrelevant factor in the real world of human need. They see the division and rivalry. So they reject it out of hand.

Others have rejected Christianity because of more personal experiences. They have had wounds inflicted on them by groups or individuals alleging to represent Jesus. In crisis situations, these people may have turned to Christians for understanding, support, and love—only to be hurt.

Take the story of Karen as a case in point. Karen is bright and articulate. She holds a degree in law and works with a respected law firm. She is married and the mother of two children, ages eleven and nine. Karen is attractive and handles practically any social situation with grace. A great many people probably envy her, and several have told her as much. But there is more to her story.

Karen has been unhappy for most of her adult life. Her own terms for describing herself are typically "restless," "frustrated," or "confused." And when someone speaks of her with respect or says something like "I really admire you," it can send her into depression. "If they only knew," she says, "they'd never look at me and think they would like to swap places." Karen, you see, has a congenital spinal defect that causes her constant back pain. And her husband is an alcoholic.

Over the past few years, this thirty-seven-year-old woman has tried several things in an effort to deal with her situation. Among the things she has tried was a brief affair with a younger man in the law firm where she works. Following that six-month affair, she went for counseling to the pastor of the church in which she had been raised by devout parents.

Karen received a stern lecture about the sin of adultery. According to the pastor, her sin was laid to the fact that she had not been attending church regularly. So she was urged to get back into church, to enroll her children in Sunday school, and to pray for her husband's recovery from alcoholism. In fewer than forty-five minutes, the preacher had heard a complex story and offered a simplistic solution. He dismissed her from his office rather formally—never following up on the conversation, never putting her in touch with resources appropriate to her needs, never communicating to her the compassion of Jesus.

If the personal problems in Karen's life smack of the intellectual issues raised earlier in this book as "the problem of evil", what she needed at the time was not rational guidance in sorting through their logical implications but real help. The failure of Christians to provide practical benefit for their neighbors who are hurting can seldom be overcome with arguments and proofs that appeal to logic.

Televangelism scandals. Unethical fund-raising. Hypocrisy. Bombing abortion clinics "in the name of God." These are not rational arguments against the Christian faith, but they nonetheless disallow faith for many. Church politics. Gossip. Racism. Again, they are not formal arguments against the Christian faith. But they force people into the posture of unbelief.

Christian faith is an existential matter as well as an intellectual concern. That is to say, people's hearts ultimately yield not to abstract argument but to the very personal touches of love and healing. An hour or two of scholarly discussion will not win a person whose heart is broken. Instead, a protracted and difficult period of acceptance and service by the spiritual body of Christ may be necessary. Only after one's stomach is filled, rocky marriage stabilized, alcoholism faced, or prison record accepted can a man or woman hear the message the church wants to share.

Social programs are not substitutes for preaching and defending the gospel. But the gospel has social implications that must be faced along with its intellectual content. Some of the people whom Christians have failed to reach are still unbelievers not because the gospel is not defensible, but because Christians have failed to see the whole persons with whom they were dealing. Until people who wear the name of Christ become a living demonstration of his presence in the world, facts and rational discussions about Christianity will be for nothing.

Having admitted that nonrational factors influence people's beliefs and values profoundly, the fact nevertheless remains that the Christian religion is shared through communication. There are facts to be related. There are truths to be stated and defended. There is a fundamental message about Jesus that must be told. In the final analysis, faith comes from hearing the gospel.

A Biblical Mandate

The first-century precedent for sharing the gospel is recorded in the New Testament documents. The Acts of the Apostles is particularly important in recording these episodes.

In the early part of the Acts, as the gospel was being preached among the Jews, the synagogues of the Jews were regular forums, and the characteristic feature of the presentation of Jesus was that Scripture was cited for proof and authority. As the message became a universal one, however, the approach changed. Since Gentiles did not know or accept the authority of the Old Testament, it would have been pointless to begin by quoting Scripture.

One of the more interesting cases that demonstrates this shift of methodology has to do with the experience of the apostle Paul. During an evangelistic tour, Paul arrived at Athens. While awaiting the arrival of Silas and Timothy, he did some sightseeing in the city. What he saw told him about the spiritual plight of its people. As he visited public places and walked through its streets, he became "greatly distressed to see that the city was full of idols" (Acts 17:16).

Without waiting for his co-workers to join him, Paul started a one-man ministry to Athens: "So he reasoned *in the synagogue* with the Jews and the God-fearing Greeks, as well as *in the marketplace* day by day with those who happened to be there" (Acts 17:17, italics added). From the record of what Paul did in the marketplace (cf. Acts 17:16–34), it is apparent that he did not *start* with Scripture. He began with a presentation of the true God on the basis of "natural theology" (what can be known of God apart from Scripture). With non-Jews of the first century and for the largely secularized world of today, natural theology is a necessary prelude to the Bible. One cannot learn what to do to be saved from natural theology, but this discipline sets the stage for introducing Scripture and teaching about Jesus of Nazareth.

When modern Christians think about evangelism, we almost always focus on "the synagogue"—that is, the traditional places for religious meetings where we anticipate finding people with a spiritual yearning of some sort already expressed. The approach of those presentations is modeled on the first part of Acts, where Scripture is quoted and debated. Too seldom do we think of "the marketplace"—that is, the public forums where we anticipate meeting people with secular or antireligious postures. But it is the latter group that is growing fastest, having the widest influence on our culture, and leading our culture along the downward spiral that comes of rejecting the knowledge of God. Without abandoning the synagogue, we must be more aggressively at work in the marketplace.

By all means, believers must evangelize people who come to our worship locations and exhibit an interest in spiritual matters. To confine our efforts there, however, is to be pitifully shortsighted, since it effectively isolates the church from the mainstream of our culture. We must imitate Paul and evangelize through social intercourse and in the arena of intellectual exchange. We must communicate our Christian commitment not only at prayer breakfasts but also at business luncheons, not only in religious journals but also in the secular press, not only in Christian schools but also in public schools, not only during evangelistic meetings at a church building but also in daily discipleship, which prompts service and sharing with people of all sorts within our spheres of influence.

In Paul's case at Athens, his sharing in the marketplace

led to an exchange in the Areopagus (Acts 17:19). It was an unlikely place for a Christian preacher, for the Areopagus was a center for philosophical debate. Into that arena went Paul the theist, Christian, and apostle. He discussed his view of the divine nature and purpose with Epicurean and Stoic philosophers. He quoted no Scripture, which they neither knew nor regarded as authoritative, but reasoned with them based on natural theology and his personal knowledge of Jesus of Nazareth. He didn't even sidestep so controversial a topic as the resurrection of Jesus from the dead.

Just as when he preached in the synagogue and argued his case from Scripture, Paul had mixed results. Some turned up their noses at his presentation, others expressed the desire to study further with him, and a few became believers (Acts 17:32–34).

Christians must get over our reluctance to enter the marketplace and must begin pressing the case for the saving work of Jesus Christ among our secularized contemporaries. Few of them will come to our assemblies. We must go where they are.

Armed with truth and careful scholarship, we must be willing to enter into dialogue with anyone who will join the discussion. Surrendered to Christ and filled with his Spirit, we must present the Christian faith. Praying fervently and believing in the power of the gospel, we must wait for the Christian message to have its effect. Some will sneer, and others will be only mildly curious. But some will be saved.

Conclusion

The larger task of Christian apologetics must do more than any book can do. It must address both the intellectual and personal life of each inquirer.

A book such as *Prepare to Answer* clearly assumes that the theoretical aspect of Christianity is necessary, worth careful articulation, and capable of defense. But beginning or would-be apologists who read it need to be warned that there are barriers to faith other than intellectual ones. It will help them present their case more effectively. It will also help them deal with the inevitable rejection that will come from some.

Rejection of the case for Christianity may be due neither to the message as presented nor to the manner of its presentation, but rather to a deeply established cultural bias or to a profound personal wound. In such cases of rejection, continue to befriend, show respect for, and await a later opportunity to discuss the rational issues of faith. Do not try to force the message on such individuals. That could justify the specific prejudice they already bear against Christians. Show love, gentleness, and patience.

If you have read this far as someone who has been an unbeliever, thank you for having an honest and inquiring mind. Thank you for moving beyond whatever culture-based reservations you may have about Christianity or Christians in order to explore some of the reasons Christians believe the things they do about God, Scripture, and Jesus. Please continue thinking and exploring.

For if there really is a God who cares about you, who shared your lot by living as a man among men, and who died to give you eternal life, these studies are more than intellectual exercises. They are foundation stones for a faith that is not a blind leap into the dark but a confident walk in the light.

Epilogue

This book has dealt with Christian faith. Specifically, it has offered a body of information and a series of rational arguments designed to defend the truth claims of Christianity. Finally, however, Christian faith is not a series of statements made and defended. It is personal trust in Jesus Christ. Trusting him to save us from our sin. Trusting him to give both direction and meaning to our lives. Trusting him to supply us victory over death.

As with any personal relationship, there is a subjectivity about trusting Jesus Christ as Savior and Lord that cannot be packaged as a syllogism. Though undergirded with facts and arguments, to be a "believer" is less a matter of admitting the truthfulness of statements than a matter of opening your heart and soul to another person. To say it another way, it is less a matter of the courtroom's "beyond reasonable doubt" than a matter of the lover's "I do."

We will not be saved by logic, argument, and proof. Salvation is not by anything that originates with us. It comes as a gift from God: "For it is by grace you have been saved, through faith—and this not from yourselves, it is the gift of God—not by works, so that no one can boast" (Eph. 2:8–9).

What occurs in the process of salvation is described in Scripture under a variety of metaphors. Each is only a metaphor, however, and is not an explanation. The work of redemption is more complex and divine than we can understand.

The Bible speaks to the person who is enslaved by drugs, sex, or greed and represents the process as "redemption." Jesus is the One "who gave himself for us to redeem us from all wickedness and to purify for himself a people that are his very own, eager to do what is good" (Titus 2:14).

It speaks to the neglected, abused, and lonely person and depicts salvation as "adoption" into the family of God. "In love he predestined us to be adopted as his sons through Jesus Christ, in accordance with his pleasure and will" (Eph. 1:5).

Scripture addresses the defeated and broken persons who see no way to resolve the chaos of their lives and weep for the chance to start over with a clean slate. It describes salvation as being "born again."

> But when the kindness and love of God our Savior appeared, he saved us, not because of righteous things we had done, but because of his mercy. He saved us through the washing of rebirth and renewal by the Holy Spirit, whom he poured out on us generously through Jesus Christ our Savior (Titus 3:4–6; cf. John 3:1ff).

The ultimate purpose of *Prepare to Answer* will be achieved only if it helps some individual move from unbelief to salvation. To sonship. To new life in Christ.

Endnotes

Chapter 1

1. George H. Smith, *Atheism: The Case Against God* (Los Angeles: Nash Publishing, 1974), xi.

2. "'Creationism' in Court," *Wall Street Journal*, 7 Jan. 1982, 16.

3. "Defenders of the Faith," *Time*, 12 Nov. 1984, 112.

4. Smith, *Atheism*, x.

5. Paul C. W. Davies, *God and the New Physics* (New York: Simon & Schuster, 1983), 102.

6. Richard L. Purtill, *Reason to Believe* (Grand Rapids: William B. Eerdmans, 1974), 18.

7. William K. Clifford, "The Ethics of Belief," in *The Rationality of Belief in God*, ed. George I. Mavrodes (Englewood Cliffs, N.J.: Prentice-Hall, 1970), 159.

8. Lewis Carroll, *Through the Looking-Glass and What Alice Found There*, in *The Complete Illustrated Works of Lewis Carroll*, ed. Edward Guiliano (New York: Avenell Books, 1982), 127–28.

Chapter 2

1. A third possible answer to the question of explaining an external world is that it doesn't really exist at all but is only an illusion. This "answer" need not concern us, for it merely reduces to one of the other possibilities in the following way: If there is no material world external to my mind, then my mind itself is the only object of real existence—yet that object (my mind) must have been either created by someone or something other than itself *or* is somehow eternal and self-explanatory under natural law.

2. *The Holy Bible*: Genesis 1:1.

3. Carl Sagan, *Cosmos* (New York: Random House, 1980), 4.

4. Any detailed discussion of the theory of evolution and its relationship to belief in God will be deferred until chapter 3. If the very existence of Planet Earth as a receptacle for life is inexplicable without appeal to an agent of creative power, the issue of how life has arisen and developed on the planet is not only premature but also moot at this stage.

5. Paul C. W. Davies, *The Accidental Universe* (London: Cambridge University Press, 1982), vii.

6. Davies, Ibid., 77.

7. Davies, Ibid., 123.

8. Davies, Ibid., viii.

9. Davies, Ibid., 123.

10. James Lovelock and Sidney Epton, "The Quest for Gaia," *New Scientist* 6 (Feb. 1975): 304.

11. F. R. Tennant, *Philosophical Theology*, vol. 2 (Cambridge: The University Press, 1930); pp. 79–93 of this work are reprinted in John Hick, ed., *The Existence of God* (New York: Macmillan, 1964), 120–36.

12. Quoted in Hick, *Existence of God*, 127–28.

13. Ibid., 129.

14. Freeman J. Dyson, *Disturbing the Universe* (New York: Harper & Row, 1979), 251.

15. Fred Hoyle and Chandra Wickramasinghe, *Evolution From Space* (New York: Simon & Schuster, 1981), 28.

16. Freeman J. Dyson, "Energy in the Universe," *Scientific American* 224 (Sept. 1971): 50.

17. Davies, *Accidental Universe*, 127.

18. Robert Jastrow, *God and the Astronomers* (New York: Warner Books, 1980), 111, 113.

19. Note: The occasional instance of an apparent counter-example to this law is only *apparent* rather than real. The growth of plants and animals or processes such as photosynthesis may at first seem to be examples of increasing order within a system of general entropy increase. In such cases, one is judging by an isolated system within the whole rather than by the total system. The concentration of order in a child's growth, for example, is paid for by increasing entropy within the total system as plants and animals are consumed, fossil fuels burned, etc. When a full balance sheet is drawn up, the total disorder within the system increases.

20. S. A. Bludman, "Thermodynamics and the End of a Closed Universe," *Nature* 308 (22 Mar. 1984): 322.

21. Bertrand Russell, *Why I Am Not a Christian* (New York: Simon & Schuster, 1957), 6–7.

22. Paul C. W. Davies, *God and the New Physics* (New York: Simon & Schuster, 1983), 49.

23. Edward P. Tryon, "What Made the World?" *New Scientist* 101 (8 Mar. 1984): 14–15; cf. James Trefil, "The Accidental Universe," *Science Digest* 92 (June 1984): 53–55, 100–104.

24. Note: For the critique of these options, I am indebted to John H. Hick, "Comment," *Canadian Journal of Philosophy* 1 (June 1972): 485–87. This brief article is the rejoinder to an article originally published by Hick on an aspect of the theistic question and responded to in *CJP*. Cf. John Hick, "God as Necessary Being," *Journal of Philosophy* 57 (1960): 725–34; D. R. Duff-Forbes, "Hick, Necessary Being, and the Cosmological Argument," *Canadian Journal of Philosophy* 1 (June 1972): 473–83.

25. Hick, "Comment," 486.

26. Ibid.

27. Ibid., 487.
28. Jastrow, *God and the Astronomers*, 104–6.
29. "The Man in the Water," *Time*, 25 Jan. 1982, 86.

Chapter 3

1. Colin Brown, *Philosophy and the Christian Faith* (Chicago: Inter-Varsity Press, 1969), 147.
2. Isaac Asimov, "The 'Threat' of Creationism," *New York Times Magazine*, (14 June 1981): 90.
3. Charles Darwin, *The Origin of Species*, Great Books of the Western World (Chicago: Encyclopaedia Britannica, 1952), 40.
4. Ibid., 41.
5. Stephen Jay Gould, "Evolution as Fact and Theory," *Discover* (May 1981): 37.
6. Melvin A. Cook, *Prehistory and Earth Models*, xi, quoted in James F. Coppedge, *Evolution: Possible or Impossible* (Grand Rapids: Zondervan, 1973), 184.
7. John G. Funkhouser and John J. Naughton, "Radiogenic Helium and Argon in Ultramafic Inclusions from Hawaii," *Journal of Geophysical Research* 75 (15, July 1968): 4603, cited in Ibid., 185.
8. Jacques Monod, *Chance and Necessity*, trans. Austryn Wainhouse (New York: Alfred A. Knopf, 1971; Vintage Books, 1972), 144.
9. Fred Hoyle, *The Intelligent Universe* (New York: Holt, Rinehart & Winston, 1983), 11–12.
10. Francis Hitching, *The Neck of the Giraffe: Where Darwin Went Wrong* (New Haven: Ticknor & Fields, 1982), 67.
11. Richard Lewontin, "Adaption," *Scientific American* (Sept. 1978): 119–30.
12. Hitching, *Neck of the Giraffe*, 86–87.
13. Ibid., 87.
14. Alan Hayward, *God Is* (Nashville: Thomas Nelson, 1978), 107.

Chapter 4

1. David Hume, *Dialogues Concerning Natural Religion*, ed. Norman Kemp Smith (New York: Thomas Nelson & Sons, 1947; Library of Liberal Arts, 1979), 196.
2. Hume, Dialogues Concerning Natural Religion, p. 198.
3. J. L. Mackie, "Evil and Omnipotence," in *God and Evil*, ed. Nelson Pike (Englewood Cliffs, N.J.: Prentice-Hall, 1964), 47.
4. Thomas Aquinas, *Summa Theologica* I. 25. 3. For a detailed discussion of the matter of defining omnipotence, cf. George Mavrodes, "Some Puzzles Concerning Omnipotence," *Philosophical Review* 72 (1963): 221–23.
5. Bruce Reichenbach, "Natural Evils and Natural Laws: A Theodicy for Natural Evils," *International Philosophical Quarterly* 16 (1976): 181. Much of the discussion of this third element of a successful theodicy draws heavily on Reichenbach's article.
6. Of course, another possibility is a world in which every event is a miraculous occurrence. Here, there would never be a connection between events and their consequences. The objection about to be formulated against regular inter-

240 Prepare to Answer

vention by miraculous power would be even more severe against such a state of affairs. For this reason, no separate point will be made of this possibility.

7. Reichenbach, "Natural Evils and Natural Laws," 187.

8. Alvin Plantinga, *God, Freedom, and Evil* (New York: Harper & Row, 1974), 36.

9. F. R. Tennant, *Philosophical Theology II* (Cambridge: Cambridge University Press, 1930), 199–200.

10. John Hick, *Evil and the God of Love* (London: Macmillan, 1966; Fontana Library, 1968), 360.

11. Ibid., 360–61.

12. "Circumstantial freedom" is not to be confused with "moral freedom." The latter involves making choices between right and wrong; the former simply entails the making of rational choices between live options. An example of moral freedom would be one's choice to return a valuable item to its rightful owner or to keep it for himself. An example of circumstantial freedom would be one's choice between driving or flying to a vacation spot.

Chapter 5

1. Quoted in *Christianity Today*, 6 Aug. 1982, 13. Italics added.

2. Benjamin B. Warfield, *The Inspiration and Authority of the Bible* (Philadelphia: Presbyterian and Reformed Pub., 1948), 442.

3. "The Bible: The Believers Gain," *Time*, 30 Dec. 1974, 34.

4. Ibid., 41.

5. James Mann, "New Finds Cast Fresh Light on the Bible," *U.S. News & World Report*, 24 Aug. 1981, 38.

6. Nelson Glueck, *Rivers in the Desert: History of Negev* (Philadelphia: Jewish Publications Society of America, 1969), 31.

7. Alan Millard, "Daniel and Belshazzar in History," *Biblical Archaeology Review* 11 (May/June 1985): 75.

8. Ibid., 77.

9. William Mitchell Ramsay, *The Bearing of Recent Discovery on the Trustworthiness of the New Testament* (London: Hodder and Stoughton, 1915; reprinted Grand Rapids: Baker Book House, 1953), 37–38. See W. Ward Gasque, *Sir William M. Ramsay: Archaeologist and New Testament Scholar* (Grand Rapids: Baker Book House, 1966) for an appreciative analysis of Ramsay's contributions to Lukan studies.

10. Ibid., 41.

11. Ibid., 53–78.

12. Ibid., 79–80.

13. A. N. Sherwin-White, *Roman Society and Roman Law in the New Testament* (Oxford: Clarendon Press, 1963), 189.

14. Ibid.

Chapter 6

1. C. J. Sharp, *Why We Believe* (Cincinnati: Standard Publishing, 1932), 12–13.

2. Justin, *The First Apology*, 5–6.

3. S. E. Massengill, *A Sketch of Medicine and Pharmacy,* 16; quoted in S. I. McMillen, *None of These Diseases* (Old Tappan, N.J.: Fleming H. Revell, 1963), 9.

4. R. K. Harrison, *Introduction to the Old Testament* (Grand Rapids: William B. Eerdmans, 1969), 610.

5. B. L. Gordon, *Medicine Throughout Antiquity,* quoted in Don England, *Evidences of Inspiration* (Searcy, Ark.: Privately published, 1971), 29; cf. P. Ghalioungui, *Magic and Medical Science in Ancient Egypt* (London: Hodder and Stoughton, 1963).

Chapter 7

1. R. K. Harrison, *Introduction to the Old Testament* (Grand Rapids: William B. Eerdmans, 1969), p. 212.

2. Josephus, *Against Apion* I. 8.

3. R. Laird Harris, "How Reliable Is the Old Testament Text?" in *Can I Trust the Bible?* (Chicago: Moody Press, 1963), 124.

4. Gleason L. Archer, Jr., *A Survey of Old Testament Introduction* (Chicago: Moody Press, 1964), 25.

5. H. H. Rowley, *The Old Testament in Modern Study* (Oxford: Clarendon Press, 1961), 25.

6. J. W. Roberts, "The Authenticity of the Scriptures," in *Pillars of Faith,* ed. Herman O. Wilson and Morris M. Womack (Grand Rapids: Baker Book House, 1973), 144.

7. Bruce M. Metzger, *The Text of the New Testament,* 2d ed. (Oxford: Oxford University Press, 1968).

8. F. F. Bruce, *The New Testament Documents: Are They Reliable?* 5th rev. ed. (Grand Rapids: William B. Eerdmans, 1971), 16–17.

9. Frederic G. Kenyon, *The Bible and Archaeology* (New York: Harper and Bros., 1940), 288.

10. Roberts, "The Authenticity of the Scriptures," 147.

11. Neil R. Lightfoot, *How We Got the Bible* (Grand Rapids: Baker Book House, 1972), p. 39. The student interested in a readable and reliable source of more information on the transmission and translation of the Bible should read this book in its entirety.

Chapter 8

1. Stephen T. Davis, *The Debate About the Bible* (Philadelphia: Westminster Press, 1977), 116.

2. John A. T. Robinson, *Can We Trust the New Testament?* (Grand Rapids: William B. Eerdmans, 1977), 36.

3. Josephus, *Antiquities* 18.1.1.

4. Note: The Greek text of Luke 2:2 does not assign a title to Quirinius. It says only that these things happened when "Quirinius controlled Syria." This is an instance where most translations obscure the reading of the original-language text.

5. Adolf Deissmann, *Light From the Ancient East* (New York: Doran Pub., 1922), 271.

6. The data above, coupled with the fact that Herod the Great died in 4 B.C.,

places the birth of Christ somewhere between 8 and 4 B.C.—likely closer to the former date than the latter. Thus most scholars put the birth between 8 and 6 B.C. The initially perplexing matter of having Jesus born several years B.C. ("Before Christ") is resolved when one realizes that the dating system that counted from the founding of Rome was replaced by our B.C–A.D. system in the sixth Christian century. An unfortunate mistake in calculations at that juncture makes the dating of Christ's birth awkward.

7. William F. Arndt and F. Wilbur Gingrich, *A Greek-English Lexicon of the New Testament and Other Early Christian Literature*, 2d ed. revised and augmented by F. Wilbur Gingrich and Frederick W. Danker (Chicago: University of Chicago Press, 1979), s.v. *"ktaomai."*

8. Alfred Plummer, *A Critical and Exegetical Commentary on the Gospel According to S. Luke*, 5th ed. (Edinburgh: T. & T. Clark, 1922), 273; cf. Alfred Edersheim, *The Temple: Its Ministry and Services* (Reprint ed., Grand Rapids: William B. Eerdmans, 1975), 65.

Chapter 9

1. G. A. Wells, *Did Jesus Exist?* (Buffalo, N.Y.: Prometheus Books, 1975), 65.

2. Lacitus, *Annals* 15.44. Suetonius mentions this same attack on the Christians in his *Life of Nero* 16.2.

3. Suetonius, *Claudius* 25. This reference to the banishment of the Jews from Rome is background to Acts 18:2.

4. Pliny, *Epistles* 10.96.

5. Will Durant, *The Story of Civilization*, vol. 3: *Caesar and Christ* (New York: Simon & Schuster, 1944), 555.

6. Ibid., 557.

7. Josephus, *Antiquities of the Jews* 18.116–19.

8. Josephus, *Antiquities* 20.200.

9. Paul Winter, "Josephus on Jesus," *Journal of Historical Studies* 1 (1968): 289–302. A revised version of this article can be found in Emil Shurer, *The History of the Jewish People in the Age of Jesus Christ*, vol. 1, revised and edited by Geza Vermes and Fergus Millar (Edinburgh: T. & T. Clark, 1973), 428–41. Cf. F. F. Bruce, *Jesus and Christian Origins Outside the New Testament* (Grand Rapids: William B. Eerdmans, 1974), 32–53.

10. Bruce, *Jesus and Christian Origins*, 39.

11. *b Shabbath* 104b.

12. Joseph Klausner, *From Jesus to Paul*, translated from the Hebrew by William F. Stinespring (Boston: Beacon Press, 1961), 260.

13. "The Three Greatest Men of History," *Reader's Digest*, May 1935, 12.

Chapter 10

1. Conservative scholars date the Book of Isaiah in the eighth century B.C., and even the most liberal of biblical scholars would not date it later than the mid-fifth century B.C.

2. *Note:* Although an alternative to the Christian interpretation of Isaiah 53 identifies the Servant as the nation of Israel, this must be rejected for the following reasons: (1) Isaiah 49:5–6 distinguishes between the Servant and Israel; (2) the

nation of Israel was to suffer in Isaiah's time for its own sins, whereas the Servant of Isaiah 53 was to suffer as an innocent victim; (3) Israel was never a voluntary sufferer as was the Servant of this text; and (4) Israel's sufferings were not intended to atone for the sins of all men. For a fuller discussion of the identity of the Suffering Servant of Isaiah 53, one could consult a source such as Oswald T. Allis, *The Unity of Isaiah* (Philadelphia: Presbyterian and Reformed Pub., 1950), 87ff.

3. John R. W. Stott, *The Authentic Jesus* (Downers Grove, Ill.: Inter-Varsity Press, 1985), 70.

Chapter 11

1. W. A. Visser't Hooft, *No Other Name* (Philadelphia: Westminster Press, 1963), 11.

2. Porphyry, *Against the Christians* Frag. 77.

Chapter 12

1. Gregory Vlastos, "The Paradox of Socrates," in *The Philosophy of Socrates* (Garden City, N.Y.: Anchor Books, 1971), 16–17.

2. Kenneth F. W. Prior, *The Gospel in a Pagan Society* (Downers Grove, Ill.: Inter-Varsity Press, 1975), 34.

3. Ibid., 36.

4. Andre Bacard, "Humanism: An Affirmation of Life," *Free Inquiry* 4 (Winter 1984/85): 47.

5. Ibid., 49.

6. "Humanist Manifesto I" originally appeared in *The New Humanist* 6 (May/June 1933); "Humanist Manifesto II" was first published in *The Humanist* 33 (Sept./Oct. 1973). The two documents have since been reprinted in booklet form and distributed widely. "A Secular Humanist Declaration" was originally published in *Free Inquiry* 1 (Winter 1980) and later distributed in booklet form.